PLAYING HARDBALL

REAL POLITICS IN AMERICA

Series Editor: Paul S. Herrnson, *University of Maryland*

The books in this series bridge the gap between academic scholarship and the popular demand for knowledge about politics. They illustrate empirically supported generalizations from original research and the academic literature using examples taken from the legislative process, executive branch decision making, court rulings, lobbying efforts, election campaigns, political movements, and other areas of American politics. The goal of the series is to convey the best contemporary political science research has to offer in ways that will engage individuals who want to know about real politics in America.

Playing Hardball:
Campaigning for the U.S. Congress

Paul S. Herrnson
University of Maryland

Prentice
Hall

Upper Saddle River, New Jersey 07458

Library of Congress Cataloging-in-Publication Data

Herrnson, Paul S.
   Playing hardball: campaigning for the U.S. Congress/Paul S. Herrnson.
     p. cm.—(Real politics in America)
   Includes bibliographical references and index.
   ISBN 0-13-027133-0
     1. United States Congress—Elections. 2. Political campaigns—United States. I. Title.
  II. Real politics in America series.

JK1976.H473 2001
324.7'0973—dc21
                                                   00-061979

VP, Editorial director: Laura Pearson
Director of marketing: Beth Gillett Mejia
Assistant editor: Brian Prybella
Editorial assistant: Beth Murtha
Editorial/production supervision: Kari Callaghan Mazzola
Prepress and manufacturing buyer: Ben Smith
Electronic page makeup: Kari Callaghan Mazzola and John P. Mazzola
Interior design: John P. Mazzola
Cover director: Jayne Conte
Cover design: Kiwi Design
Cover photo: PhotoDisc, Inc.

This book was set in 10/12 Palatino by Big Sky Composition
and was printed and bound by Courier Companies, Inc.
The cover was printed by Phoenix Color Corp.

Real Politics in America
Series Editor: Paul S. Herrnson

Printed in the United States of America
10 9 8 7 6 5 4 3 2 1

ISBN 0-13-027133-0

PRENTICE-HALL INTERNATIONAL (UK) LIMITED, *London*
PRENTICE-HALL OF AUSTRALIA PTY. LIMITED, *Sydney*
PRENTICE-HALL CANADA INC., *Toronto*
PRENTICE-HALL HISPANOAMERICANA, S.A., *Mexico*
PRENTICE-HALL OF INDIA PRIVATE LIMITED, *New Delhi*
PRENTICE-HALL OF JAPAN, INC., *Tokyo*
PEARSON EDUCATION ASIA PTE. LTD., *Singapore*
EDITORA PRENTICE-HALL DO BRASIL, LTDA., *Rio de Janeiro*

CONTENTS

Chapter 4

Chapter 5

Chapter 6

Chapter 7

PREFACE

This volume examines the most important aspects of congressional election campaigns, ranging from the decision to run to campaign strategy to political reform. It consists of a collection of cutting-edge studies written by scholars who are experts in campaigns and elections. Many of the authors have had significant experience working in political campaigns. The studies use new data sets to analyze candidate emergence, campaign fundraising, strategy, television advertising, and fieldwork. They combine quantitative data analysis with descriptions and examples drawn from real politics. Collectively, they document some of the underlying biases in the contemporary election system; analyze their implications for campaigns waged by challengers, incumbents, and candidates for open seats; and explore the prospects for reform.

Contemporary political science scholarship lays a firm foundation for comprehending the underlying dynamics of congressional elections, but it could be more successful in presenting this information to students and the general public. Results generated from formal models, statistical analyses, case studies, and systematic comparisons—the basic tools of the discipline—are often not accessible to practitioners or the general reader. In congressional elections, it is not always possible to explain campaign decision making using any one of these approaches. It is also unwise to try to interpret the decisions of voters without first examining the efforts of campaigners who seek to influence their vote. Candidates and potential candidates, donors and potential donors, campaign strategists and communications experts possess a variety of goals, perspectives, and views about what are appropriate tactics in congressional elections. The best way to examine congressional election campaigns is from the inside out, first by examining the motives and goals of those who participate in campaigns, next by analyzing how they mount their campaign efforts, and only after that assessing the campaigns' impact on contributors and voters.

The chapters that follow bridge the gap between academic scholarship and the popular demand for knowledge about politics. The goal of this book is to provide readers with a manageable perspective on congressional elections and real life American politics, enhancing their ability to make the connections between the theory and practice of politics. The chapters illustrate empirically supported generalizations from original research and the academic literature using examples taken from the electoral process. The decisions of individuals who participate in campaigns can have tremendous consequences for Americans and citizens of other nations. The same is true of the officials they elected, party leaders, interest group lobbyists, voters, and protesters who try to influence the actions of those in government.

This volume could not have been completed without the assistance of many individuals and organizations. First and foremost, thanks are due to the scholars who contributed the chapters. They tolerated my exhortations to put aside the "rules" of writing they learned in graduate school, to make their chapters interesting and accessible to a broad audience, and to give readers a sense of what it is like to participate in real politics. Next, I wish to thank Beth Gillett Mejia of Prentice Hall, Kari Callaghan Mazzola of Big Sky Composition, and Virginia Rubens for transforming the manuscript into a book. Finally, I wish to thank The Pew Charitable Trusts for sponsoring the Campaign Emergence and Candidate Outreach Project, which funded much of the research presented in this volume. The opinions expressed in this book are those of the authors and do not necessarily reflect the views of The Pew Charitable Trusts.

Paul S. Herrnson

About the Contributors

Owen G. Abbe is a Ph.D. candidate in government and politics at the University of Maryland. His research interests include electoral politics and campaign finance at both the national and state levels. His dissertation is entitled "The Nationalization of State Campaign Finance: Out-of-State Influence in the 1996 State Legislative Elections."

Lee Bradford received his B.A. in political science from Otterbein College and his M.A., also in political science, from Arizona State University. His research interests are in mediated politics. He currently works for the Campaign Media Analysis Group in Alexandria, Virginia.

Peter L. Francia is currently a research fellow at the Center for American Politics and Citizenship at the University of Maryland. His research interests include elections, campaign finance, and labor unions and politics. He has published several articles and book chapters on these subjects.

Ken Goldstein is assistant professor of political science at the University of Wisconsin–Madison. He earned his Ph.D. in political science at the University of Michigan in 1996. He is the author of *Interest Groups, Lobbying, and Participation in America*. His research on political advertising, turnout, campaign finance, survey methodology, and presidential elections has appeared in the *American Journal of Political Science*, the *Journal of Politics*, and *Public Opinion Quarterly*, as well as in a series of book chapters. He is currently at work on a book project on television advertising. Goldstein also has an interest in Israeli politics and is currently working on a project on the political socialization and behavior of immigrants from the former Soviet Union.

JOHN C. GREEN is director of the Ray C. Bliss Institute of Applied Politics and professor of political science at the University of Akron. He has done extensive research on campaign finance and religion and politics. Most recently he edited *Financing the 1996 Election* and is the coauthor of *The Diminishing Divide: Religion's Changing Role in American Politics*.

MICHAEL T. HANNAHAN is an assistant professor at the University of Massachusetts at Amherst. Professor Hannahan received his B.A. from Miami University of Ohio and his M.A. in public administration and Ph.D. from the University of Massachusetts. In addition to teaching political science, Dr. Hannahan is the vice president of Voter Contact Services, the nation's largest supplier of direct contact materials to political campaigns. He has been a State Party Executive Director and a political consultant.

PAUL S. HERRNSON is director of the Center for American Politics and Citizenship and professor of government and politics at the University of Maryland. He is the author of *Congressional Elections: Campaigning at Home and in Washington* and *Party Campaigning in the 1980s*. He has published numerous articles and book chapters on political parties, interest groups, Congress, and elections. Professor Herrnson is a former American Political Science Association Congressional Fellow and is the recipient of several teaching awards. He received his B.A. from the State University of New York at Binghamton and his Ph.D. from the University of Wisconsin–Madison.

JONATHAN S. KRASNO is a Senior Research Fellow at the Center for American Politics and Citizenship at the University of Maryland. His major research interests include political campaigns, campaign finance, and congressional elections. He is the author of *Buying Time: Television Advertising in the 1998 Congressional Elections* and *Challengers, Competition, and Reelection: Comparing Senate and House Elections*. He earned a Ph.D. in political science from the University of California, Berkeley.

CHERIE MAESTAS is an assistant professor of political science at Texas Tech University. She has published articles on state legislatures, legislative behavior, and political methodology in *Legislative Studies Quarterly* and *Electoral Studies*. Currently, she is studying the role of political ambition in representation, the effect of uncertainty on incumbent behavior, and candidate emergence in U.S. House elections.

DAVID B. MAGLEBY is nationally recognized for his expertise on direct democracy, voting behavior, and campaign finance. He received his B.A. from the University of Utah in 1973 and his Ph.D. from the University of California, Berkeley. He is currently Distinguished Professor of Political Science at Brigham Young University. His writings include *Direct Legislation* (1984), *The Money Chase: Congressional Campaign Finance Reform* (1990), *The Myth of the*

Independent Voter (1992), several editions of an American government text-book, *Government by the People*, and, most recently, *Outside Money: Money and Issue Advocacy in the 1998 Congressional Elections* (2000). A past-president of Pi Sigma Alpha, the national political science honor society, he has also published numerous articles in political science journals.

L. SANDY MAISEL is the William R. Kanan Jr. Professor of Government at Colby College in Waterville, Maine, where he has taught courses on American government for thirty years. His most recent books include *Parties and Elections in America: The Electoral Process*, now in its third edition, and *Two Parties—Or More? The American Party System* (with John Bibby). He has edited three volumes of *The Parties Respond* and is series editor for the *Dilemmas in American Politics* series with Westview Press. With Walter Stone, he is co-principal investigator for the Candidate Emergence Project, from which the chapter in this book emanates.

KELLY D. PATTERSON is an associate professor in the Department of Political Science at Brigham Young University. He is the author of *Political Parties and the Maintenance of Liberal Democracy* (1996). His teaching and research interests include political parties, campaigns and elections, and theories of American politics. He is a former American Political Science Association Congressional Fellow.

LYNDA W. POWELL is professor of political science at the University of Rochester. She is coauthor of *Serious Money: Fundraising and Contributing in Presidential Nomination Campaigns*, and has published articles on women in politics, campaign contributors, congressional and presidential elections, and congressional representation.

DANIEL E. SELTZ was a researcher and project coordinator at the Brennan Center for Justice at New York University School of Law from 1998 to 2000. Before joining the Brennan Center, he was a Fulbright Fellow at Hiroshima University. His writing has appeared in *Radical History Review* and *Hiroshima Peace Science* (in Japanese).

WALTER J. STONE is professor of political science at the University of Colorado, where he has taught since 1982. He is the author of *Republic at Risk: Self Interest in American Politics* (1990) and coauthor of *Nomination Politics: Party Activists and Presidential Choice* (1984). He was the editor of the *Political Research Quarterly* (1989–1995). He has published numerous articles on the American party system, political representation, legislative politics, and electoral politics, and is currently engaged in two collaborative projects, both supported by grants by the National Science Foundation: The Candidate Emergence Study (with L. Sandy Maisel) and a study of the Perot movement and major-party change (with Ronald B. Rapoport).

BEN WEBSTER is a Ph.D. candidate in the Government Department at Georgetown University. His research focuses on environmental policy, specifically the interaction between the federal judiciary, Congress, and the EPA.

CLYDE WILCOX is professor of government at Georgetown University. He is the author or editor of many books and articles on gender politics, religion and politics, and campaign finance. He is coauthor of *Serious Money: Fundraising and Contributing in Presidential Nomination Campaigns,* and is currently collaborating on a book on congressional campaign contributors.

PLAYING HARDBALL

1

INTRODUCTION

PAUL S. HERRNSON

Congressional elections are the ultimate in hardball politics. Members of Congress and those who want to join their ranks must compete for a limited number of positions, and there can be only one winner at the end of each campaign. Races are run on a field that is designed to advantage incumbents over all others. Campaigning places tremendous stresses on candidates' personal and professional lives. The costs of entering and staying in the game are high in terms of money, commitment, and energy. Moreover, many of the political consultants who coach the candidates maintain that playing dirty—including attacking an opponent personally—is necessary to win.

For at least some successful candidates, the thrill of victory is diminished by the need to continue to raise money in order to pay off campaign debts. The knowledge that in a few months they will need to begin repeating the cycle of fund-raising and meeting with voters weighs heavily on the minds of at least some House members. Of course, winning is better than suffering the agony of defeat. Losing can be a tremendous letdown to candidates and campaign aides who have spent months—sometimes years—focusing on the election. Moreover, the immediate impact of losing is frequently compounded by the fact that an individual may have given up some other office in order to run for Congress. The possibility of finding oneself unemployed is occasionally accompanied by the belief that the current loss may have effectively ended the candidate's political career.

There are some organizations that reward those who have put in years of faithful service with a gold watch. Congress is not one of them. The "reward" that defeated members of Congress and other losing candidates receive is the humiliation that accompanies public rejection at the polls. It is a wonder that individuals are willing to subject themselves to the trials of a congressional race at all.

1

Why do people run for Congress, and what impact does the uneven playing field have on the decisions of potential candidates? Who finances congressional campaigns, and what effects does incumbency have on fund-raising? Who assists candidates in their bids for office, and what effect does the staffing of campaigns have on the strategies and tactics that candidates use? How negative is television advertising in congressional elections? Are the candidates the culprits behind televised attack advertising, or are political parties also culpable? How important are less visible, more highly targeted forms of voter contact? What kinds of voters do campaigns target for direct-mail or telemarketing, and how do their targeting choices influence who ultimately votes? What are the implications of these different aspects of congressional elections for governance? What are the prospects for reform? Following a brief overview of the congressional election system, this book presents six original essays that examine these and related questions.

THE RULES OF THE GAME

Congressional elections are similar to most other aspects of democratic government in that campaigns are governed by sets of laws, rules, and norms. The Constitution requires that all House members be U.S. citizens, 25 years of age or older, and reside in the states they represent. The Apportionment Act of 1842 requires that House members be elected from single-member, winner-take-all districts.[1] The Federal Election Campaign Act of 1974 and its amendments (collectively known as FECA) limit the amounts of money that candidates can accept from individuals, party committees, and interest-group political action committees (PACs). However, parties, PACs, and individuals can make unlimited independent expenditures that *expressly* advocate the election or defeat of specific candidates using "hard" money that is collected, disbursed, and reported in compliance with the FECA. Parties and other interest groups, including corporations, trade associations, and unions, can also spend unlimited amounts of "soft" money raised outside of the FECA's regulatory regime to influence congressional elections as long as they spend it on communications that do not expressly advocate a candidate's election or defeat.[2] Many of these so-called "issue advocacy ads" resemble candidate ads, but they tend to be more negative in content.[3]

Other laws governing the electoral participation of candidates and voters, including the configuration of congressional districts and who is eligible to vote in congressional nominating contests and general elections, are set by individual states. Whether voters can cast their ballots by mail or are required to appear at a polling place in person is also determined by each state. The states, which actually administer congressional primaries, also regulate some aspects of these nomination contests.

Party organizations have varying degrees of freedom to create rules that govern how congressional nominating contests are waged. In most states, parties select their congressional nominees in primaries, but a few use caucuses or some combination of a caucus, convention, or primary. Other party rules, codified into law in some states, determine who can participate in a congressional nominating contest. In some states, participation is limited to individuals who have registered as party members. In others, both party registrants and independent voters can participate. In still others, anyone who is registered to vote can participate in a party's primary, including voters who are registered members of another party.

Federal statutes, state laws, and party rules are not the only factors that influence the conduct of congressional elections. Societal norms and expectations and the distribution of wealth also have an impact on congressional elections. Despite a trend toward greater diversity in its membership, it is no mere accident that most members of Congress are politically moderate, well-educated, financially advantaged white males who have previous political experience and are affiliated with either the Democratic or Republican parties. Disproportionate numbers from this group run for Congress, and they possess many of the skills, financial resources, time, and connections needed to mount a successful campaign.[4] Voters are biased in favor of casting ballots for candidates who belong to this group.[5]

The rules of the game apply to all candidates equally, but they are by no means neutral. They advantage some potential and actual candidates over others. The rules create an uneven playing field that favors incumbents over challengers, wealthy candidates over poor ones, and major-party contestants over independents and minor-party candidates. The rules have an impact on who runs for Congress and on the activities of the political consultants, parties, and others that participate in congressional campaigns.

THE PLAYERS

The rules of the game have resulted in the development of a candidate-centered congressional election system. In the United States, candidates, not parties, are the locus of most campaign activity. Political parties may influence the decisions of some potential candidates, but they have far less influence on candidate recruitment in the United States than they have in most other industrialized democracies. Candidates, not parties, also are responsible for mounting campaigns in the United States, whereas the opposite is true in most other democratic nations. Indeed, congressional candidates must raise their own funds, hire their own political aides and consultants, formulate their own voter contact and communications strategies, and bear the overall responsibility for their campaigns. For the most part, only those who have been successful at this receive significant party help.

Paid campaign aides and political consultants constitute central elements of most House candidates' campaign teams. Most incumbents assemble a highly professional campaign organization, drawing on the services of professional managers, fund-raisers, pollsters, issue and opposition researchers, direct-mail experts, media consultants, press aides, and accountants. Approximately 45 percent even contract for the services of an attorney to keep them from running afoul of the law. Challengers' campaign organizations are significantly less professional, but a majority of all challengers pay a campaign aide or a consultant to manage their campaigns, carry out their fundraising, serve as liaisons to the media, and design their communications. Open-seat campaigns are roughly as professional as the campaign teams put together by incumbents, but they are significantly less likely to keep an attorney on retainer.[6]

Political parties play important supplemental roles in congressional elections, especially in competitive contests. They encourage some candidates to run while discouraging others. They also provide some candidates with contributions, coordinated expenditures, volunteers, and election services that often take the form of strategic advice, polls, issue or opposition research, media buys, and fund-raising help. Party assistance can be critical in enabling a candidate to raise money, hire consultants, and attract media attention. Some candidates are the beneficiaries of party independent expenditures, issue advocacy ads, and voter mobilization efforts. Candidates competing in hotly contested races are the major beneficiaries of party assistance, and party help typically has its biggest impact on campaigns waged by nonincumbents.[7]

Interest groups, particularly PACs, are an important source of money in congressional elections. PACs accounted for approximately 40 percent of the resources raised by a typical House incumbent in a contested election in 1998, about 15 percent of the funds raised by challengers, and almost one-quarter of the money collected by open-seat candidates. Most business-oriented PACs give the vast majority of their contributions to incumbents because they are interested in obtaining the access needed to influence the legislative process.[8] For that reason, members of Congress who hold congressional leadership posts or serve on important policy-making committees are able to raise the most PAC money.[9] Ideological PACs, which champion causes such as abortion rights, family values, and other visceral issues, are more likely than access-oriented PACs to contribute to competitive nonincumbents.[10] These PACs make campaign contributions to help elect legislators who are sympathetic to their cause, as opposed to making them to encourage an incumbent to return their lobbyist's telephone call. A final group of PACs use aspects of both strategies when making contributions. Most labor-union PACs, for example, give more than 90 percent of their contributions to Democratic candidates because they agree with the candidate's ideology, but they distribute a large portion of these contributions to Democratic Party and committee leaders who hold safe seats in order to influence the legislative process.[11] In addition to making PAC contributions, some interest groups provide candidates with campaign services similar to those distributed by parties and make independent expenditures and issue ads to try to influence the outcome of congressional elections.[12]

The mass media constitute an important set of players in congressional elections, despite the fact that some candidates and many voters consider the media little more than a tool for conveying information. Candidates can communicate with voters in three ways: by spending their own funds on television, radio, direct-mail, brochures, fieldwork, and other advertisements; by motivating parties and interest groups to communicate their message for them; and by encouraging journalists to write favorable stories about their candidacies or campaigns. Free media, also known as earned media, has the advantage of costing the candidate little in terms of campaign expenditures, but it has the disadvantage of not being under the candidate's control. Just as a good interview, a well-staged press conference, a strong showing in a debate, or a pithy media advisory can result in a candidate's receiving a great deal of favorable free publicity, a poor performance in any one of these arenas can result in a publicity nightmare. Perhaps even worse than bad coverage, particularly for a congressional challenger, is no coverage at all. For that reason, shrewd candidates and their staffs cultivate good relations with members of the so-called fourth estate and provide them with a steady stream of timely, newsworthy information about their campaigns.[13]

Cynics believe that the primary role of voters is to be manipulated by candidates and campaigns, but, in fact, politically active citizens play important roles in congressional elections. Individuals usually account for at least half of the money raised by general election candidates for the House. Individual contributions also constitute an important source of seed money that candidates use to raise more funds.[14] In addition, politically active citizens are an important source of campaign support. Many campaigns rely on volunteers for accounting services and legal advice and to help with fundraising, campaign management, and many other essential campaign activities. Roughly half of all House campaigns rely on volunteers to carry on grass-roots activities, such as registration and get-out-the-vote drives. Challengers, who typically assemble the least professional campaign organizations, depend most heavily on volunteers to help them wage their campaigns, but few incumbents have difficulty convincing volunteers to assist them with their reelection efforts.[15]

STRATEGIES

Running for Congress is a monumental task for any candidate, but it is especially difficult for a challenger. Congressional elections take place on a playing field that advantages incumbents. Incumbents are usually well-known and popular among their constituents, sometimes enjoying celebrity status. They are able to raise large amounts of campaign money and attract media coverage, and they possess the wherewithal to assemble professional campaign organizations and attract campaign volunteers. With incumbency comes the benefits of experience, including knowledge of the issues, well-honed public speaking and debating abilities, and a well-formulated sense of what does and does not work in a political campaign. Incumbents also benefit from the fact that most voters in their districts are used to supporting them at the polls. As a result of these advantages, and the corresponding disadvantages of House challengers, reelection rates for incumbents are typically above 90 percent.

Challengers are more often than not in the opposite position of incumbents. With the exception of actors, athletes, and other celebrities, most challengers begin their quest for a House seat in obscurity.[16] Most challengers also begin and end their campaigns short on cash and unable to attract much attention from the media. Their relative inexperience, inability to contract the services of experienced political consultants, and lack of support from party committees, PACs, and other interest groups destines most challengers to lose their races. Even the relatively few challengers who are able to mount campaigns resembling those waged by incumbents usually lose anyway because most of the voters in their districts are in the habit of supporting the incumbent. When a challenger asks voters for their ballots, he or she is in essence asking those people to fire the incumbent. Most people have difficulty firing others.

Open-seat contests are usually the most competitive. With neither general election candidate enjoying the advantages of incumbency, both candidates usually have a reasonable expectation that they can win. More important, so do the individuals and organizations that work on, volunteer for, contribute to, and report about campaigns. The incumbency cue, which dominates individuals' voting decisions in most congressional elections that feature a sitting House member, is not present. This results in some voters' falling back on the candidates' party affiliations when making their voting decisions, but it encourages others to make a conscious attempt to weigh the assets and liabilities of each candidate.[17] Moreover, heightened competition generally encourages voters to be more attuned to the campaign and encourages higher election turnout.[18]

Virtually all congressional candidates wage what are essentially two campaigns, each of which is designed to collect some of the ingredients necessary for victory. The campaign for votes takes place in the district and is designed to mobilize the candidate's base and win the support of undecided or "swing" voters. The campaign for money, election services, and other forms of campaign support takes place primarily in Washington, New York, Hollywood, and the nation's other financial and political centers. Because they begin at different starting points, incumbents, challengers, and open-seat candidates usually employ different campaign strategies and tactics.[19]

Incumbent strategies are designed to capitalize on the advantages of holding office. Incumbents begin fund-raising early, sometimes only weeks after the previous election and almost always before an opponent declares his or her intention to run. They also use their political clout to convince PACs and individuals interested in gaining access to make contributions. Those in close races can use their voting records to attract the support of ideologically motivated donors. Most incumbent solicitations highlight their influence in the policy-making process and their accomplishments in office. Incumbent fund-raising is frequently driven by the threat posed by a potential or actual opponent.[20] Incumbents who face strong challenges raise large sums, feverishly collecting it throughout the election season. Those who do not, usually raise substantial sums early, and their fund-raising efforts drop off once they realize they face only weak competition.

Incumbent campaigns for votes typically highlight the candidate's public persona and accomplishments in office. Most House members disseminate messages that reinforce the same imagery, themes, and issue positions that they highlight in their newsletters, constituent mail, and personal appearances around the district. These frequently portray the member as tirelessly working to get constituents' views heard in the Capitol, ensure that the district receives its fair share of federal projects, and resolve conflicts that arise between constituents and the federal government. Incumbents who have only recently been elected to the House tend to focus primarily on how well they serve the district; those who have served many terms discuss the benefits that their constituents derive from being represented by a congressional leader. Incumbents know who most of their supporters are and where they live. They direct their campaign communications and voter mobilization efforts to parts of the district that have previously supported them.[21]

Challengers' relative invisibility in their districts means that they have the most to gain from raising and spending campaign money.[22] Nevertheless, challengers raise the least of any group of candidates. There are many reasons for this. Most begin fund-raising relatively late in the game, including those who begin fund-raising less than a year before election day. Challengers also have none of the fund-raising clout that comes with incumbency, and most politically aware donors know that challengers have extremely long odds of winning. This makes it difficult for them to raise contributions from access-oriented PACs and individuals. Challengers in competitive races, however, can usually raise some funds from ideological donors who share their policy views; but even these amounts are miniscule compared with those raised by incumbents. As a result, challengers' campaign war chests are typically only about one-third the size of those of their opponents.

Their lack of campaign funds, limited visibility, and need to attract the support of individuals who have not previously voted for them influence how challengers communicate with voters. Challengers need to give most voters a reason to shift their loyalties away from the incumbent and vote for someone new. Many challengers seek to do this by using policy issues and their political or personal experiences to distinguish themselves from the incumbent. Most challengers also attack weaknesses in their opponent's congressional voting record, claim that their opponent has failed to adequately represent constituency interests, or use broad-brushed attacks to tie the incumbent to unpopular federal programs, policies, or perceptions of government corruption. A lack of campaign funds encourages challengers to rely less on television and more on campaign literature, speeches, debates, and other low-budget methods of campaign communications.[23] Challengers also have to work harder to obtain free media, since most maintain that journalists favor incumbents when reporting about politics.[24] Given that most factors work so strongly against them, it is unusual for a challenger to wage a highly competitive race, and even more unusual for one of them to win.

Candidates for open seats are usually very successful at raising campaign funds. Because their elections tend to be competitive, both candidates in an open-seat contest can usually raise substantial resources. Most open-seat candidates also have had some form of political experience and can use their political record to raise money from donors who are motivated by specific issues or ideology. Open-seat candidates raise fewer PAC dollars and are substantially less dependent on these organizations than are incumbents, but they raise PAC money and depend on it more heavily than do challengers.

Similarly, most open-seat candidates enjoy rough parity with their opponents when it comes to attracting voter support and media attention. Voters who had habitually cast their ballots for the incumbent are more receptive to campaign communications urging them to vote for someone else, though many may be unwilling to cross party lines when casting their ballots. Journalists are more likely to give both candidates similar amounts of news coverage. Campaign advertising and mobilization efforts play a larger role in determining the outcomes of these races than they do in other contests.

THE GAME PLAN FOR THE BOOK

The chapters that follow examine candidate emergence, campaign organization and strategy, fund-raising, television advertising, direct mail, and election outcomes. The first three chapters are devoted to the decision to run for Congress, fund-raising, campaign organization, and strategy. In Chapter 2, Sandy Maisel, Walter Stone, and Cherie Maestas analyze the personal, professional, and political considerations that potential congressional candidates ponder, and the impact of these considerations on who ultimately runs and on their prospects for electoral success. Chapter 3, by Benjamin Webster, Clyde Wilcox, Paul Herrnson, Peter Francia, John Green, and Lynda Powell, discusses inequities in campaign financing, including the amounts of money that incumbents and challengers raise; the difficulties that the latter encounter in fund-raising; differences in sources of challengers' and incumbents' funds;

and the impact that money has in promoting high reelection rates. In Chapter 4, Owen Abbe, Paul Herrnson, Kelly Patterson, and David Magleby analyze the impact that political consultants have on congressional campaigns. We show that candidates who put together professional campaign organizations are more likely to attack their opponents than are candidates who wage amateur campaigns, but their attacks do not increase their probability of electoral success.

The next two chapters focus on campaign communications. In Chapter 5, Kenneth Goldstein, Jonathan Krasno, Lee Bradford, and Daniel Seltz profile the content of the television advertising used by 1998 congressional candidates, demonstrating that most candidate ads are positive or comparative rather than negative. Indeed, party committees, not candidates, were largely responsible for the mudslinging that took place in those contests. Chapter 6, by Michael Hannahan, shows that congressional campaigns use direct mail and mass telephoning primarily to contact individuals who routinely vote in congressional elections. Ironically, such contacts have a limited impact on these voters' likelihood of casting ballots; but when direct mail and telephone efforts are targeted at individuals who do not have a previous history of voting, they markedly increase the propensities of these individuals to go to the polls.

In the final chapter, I draw together the major findings of the previous chapters and discuss their implications for governance. I also explore the institutional advantages incumbents have built into the political system to help them perpetuate their hold on their congressional seats. Finally, I discuss prospects for improving the way congressional campaigns are waged.

NOTES

1. Kenneth Martis, *The Historical Atlas of U.S. Congressional Districts, 1789–1983* (New York: Free Press, 1982), 5–6.
2. For detailed coverage of the law, see Anthony Corrado, Thomas E. Mann, Daniel R. Ortiz, Trevor Potter, and Frank J. Sorauf, eds., *Campaign Finance Reform: A Sourcebook* (Washington, DC: Brookings Institution, 1997); for a useful summary see Paul S. Herrnson, *Congressional Elections: Campaigning at Home and in Washington*, 3rd ed. (Washington, DC: CQ Press, 2000), 14–19.
3. Paul S. Herrnson and Diana Dwyre, "Party Issue Advocacy in Congressional Elections," in John C. Green and Daniel M. Shea, eds., *The State of the Parties*, 3rd ed. (Lanham, MD: University of America Press, 1999), 86–104.
4. David T. Canon, *Actors, Athletes, and Astronauts: Political Amateurs in the United States* (Chicago: University of Chicago Press, 1990), 4–10; Herrnson, *Congressional Elections*, 56–62.
5. Carol K. Sigelman, Lee Sigelman, Dan B. Thomas, and Frederick D. Ribich, "Gender, Physical Attractiveness, and Electability: An Experimental Investigation of

Voter Biases," *Journal of Applied Psychology* 16 (1986): 229–248; Kim Fridkin Kahn, "Does Being Male Help? An Investigation of the Effects of Candidate Gender and Campaign Coverage on Evaluations of U.S. Senate Candidates," *Journal of Politics* 54 (1992): 497–517.

6. Herrnson, *Congressional Elections*, 71–76.
7. Herrnson, *Congressional Elections*, 111–117.
8. Richard Hall and Frank Wayman, "Buying Time: Moneyed Interests and the Mobilization of Bias in Congressional Committees," *American Political Science Review* 84 (1990): 797–820. See also the case studies in *Risky Business? PAC Decisionmaking in Congressional Elections*, ed. Robert Biersack, Paul S. Herrnson, and Clyde Wilcox (Armonk, NY: M. E. Sharpe, 1994) and *After the Revolution: PACs and Lobbies in the New Republican Congress*, ed. Robert Biersack, Paul S. Herrnson, and Clyde Wilcox (Boston: Allyn and Bacon, 1999).
9. Janet M. Grenzke, "PACs and the Congressional Supermarket: The Currency Is Complex," *American Journal of Political Science* 33 (February 1989): 1–24; John Wright, "Contributions, Lobbying, and Committee Voting in the U.S. House of Representatives," *American Political Science Review* 84 (1990): 417–438; Kevin B. Grier and Michael C. Munger, "Comparing Interest Group PAC Contributions to House and Senate Incumbents, 1980–1986," *Journal of Politics* 55 (August 1993): 615–643; Thomas Romer and James M. Snyder Jr., "An Empirical Investigation of the Dynamics of PAC Contributions," *American Journal of Political Science* 38 (1994): 745–769.
10. See the case studies in *Risky Business?* and *After the Revolution*.
11. Herrnson, *Congressional Elections*, 135–137.
12. See, for example, Linda L. Fowler and Robert D. McClure, *Political Ambition: Who Decides to Run for Congress* (New Haven: Yale University Press, 1989), 205–207; Paul S. Herrnson, "The National Committee for an Effective Congress: Ideology, Partisanship, and Electoral Innovation," in *Risky Business?*; Mark J. Rozell, "WISH List: Pro-Choice Women in the Republican Congress," in *After the Revolution*.
13. Sallie G. Randolph, "The Effective Press Release: Key to Free Media," in *Campaigns & Elections*, ed. Larry J. Sabato (Glenview, IL: Scott Foresman, 1989), 26–32; Anita Dunn, "The Best Campaign Wins: Coverage of Down Ballot Races by Local Press" (paper presented at the Conference on Campaign Management, American University, Washington, DC, December 10–11, 1992).
14. Robert Biersack, Paul S. Herrnson, and Clyde Wilcox, "Seeds for Success: Early Money in Congressional Elections," *Legislative Studies Quarterly* 18 (1993): 535–553; Jonathan S. Krasno, Donald Philip Green, and Jonathan A. Cowden, "The Dynamics of Fundraising in House Elections," *Journal of Politics* 56 (1994): 459–474.
15. Herrnson, *Congressional Elections*, 76.
16. Canon, *Actors, Athletes, and Astronauts*.
17. Morris P. Fiorina, *Retrospective Voting in American National Elections* (New Haven: Yale University Press, 1981); Raymond E. Wolfinger, "Candidates and Parties in Congressional Elections," *American Political Science Review* 74 (1980): 622–629; Barbara Hinckley, "House Re-Elections and Senate Defeats: The Role of the Challenger," *British Journal of Political Science* 10 (1980): 441–460; Gary C. Jacobson, *The Politics of Congressional Elections*, 4th ed. (New York: Longman, 1997), 106–108.
18. Robert D. Brown and James A. Woods, "Toward a Model of Congressional Elections," *Journal of Politics* 53 (1991): 454–473; John R. Zaller, *The Nature and Origins of Mass Opinion* (Cambridge, England: Cambridge University Press, 1992), ch. 10.

19. Herrnson, *Congressional Elections, passim.*
20. Gary C. Jacobson, *Money in Congressional Elections* (New Haven: Yale University Press, 1980), 113–123; Krasno, Green, and Cowden, "The Dynamics of Fundraising in House Elections."
21. Richard F. Fenno Jr., *Home Style: House Members in Their Districts* (Boston: Little, Brown, 1978), esp. chs. 3 and 4.
22. Jacobson, *The Politics of Congressional Elections*, 104–106; Christopher Kenney and Michael McBurdett, "A Dynamic Model of Congressional Spending on Vote Choice," *American Journal of Political Science* 36 (1992): 923–937; Herrnson, *Congressional Elections*, 232, 235.
23. Herrnson, *Congressional Elections*, 221–222.
24. Herrnson, *Congressional Elections*, 216–217.

2

Quality Challengers to Congressional Incumbents: Can Better Candidates Be Found?

L. SANDY MAISEL / WALTER J. STONE / CHERIE MAESTAS

By many accounts, the 1998 U.S. House elections were among the most competitive in recent history. Indeed, the election led to a distribution of seats in the House of Representatives that was the most closely divided between the parties since the first years of the Eisenhower administration. A switch of only six seats in that election from the Republicans to the Democrats would have made Richard Gephardt (D-MO) Speaker of the House and Dennis Hastert (R-IL), or whomever the Republicans chose as their leader, minority leader. Political observers were well aware of the stakes involved in the 1998 election; while the Democratic gains were unexpected, the Republicans had entered the contest with only a 19-seat cushion from the 105th Congress.

So the election of 1998 was hotly contested. Or was it? In fact, in that election 94 seats went to one major party or the other without any challenge from the other major party. In each of those cases, an incumbent was reelected with no major-party opposition at all. Another 39 incumbents, out of approximately 400 seeking reelection, won with over 75 percent of the vote, indicating that the opposition was minimal. Only 30 of the incumbents seeking reelection polled less than 55 percent of the vote in 1998; 5 of those 30 lost. In a very real sense, then, little or no competition marked the 1998 congressional elections in the vast majority of the 400 seats in which incumbents were seeking to return to the House.

The claim that the 1998 congressional elections were hotly contested rests on the 40 to 45 seats that the two parties felt were "in play." The parties concentrated their resources on those seats, spending soft money to aid their candidates' efforts; interest groups ran "issue advocacy" ads in these districts, using every means possible to influence the results; the candidates themselves spent enormous amounts of money to capture the open seats or to oppose those few incumbents thought to be in jeopardy. At the national level, one could argue that the election was highly competitive because partisan control of the House hung in the balance. So even though the Republicans won roughly 45 percent of the seats quite easily and the Democrats won about the same number with as little trouble, the real political battle was for the remaining 10 percent of the districts. These were the seats that determined which party would control the House agenda.

Without discounting that logic, we are left to wonder about the 90 percent of the seats that were not tightly contested. Were there no qualified candidates in those districts who were willing to take on incumbents? Were many incumbents given a free ride unnecessarily? What kinds of potential candidates chose *not* to run in 1998? In this chapter we focus on one aspect of the lack of competition: the missing players in 1998—the potential House candidates who weren't actually candidates because they decided *not* to run in 1998.

THE IMPORTANCE OF QUALITY CANDIDATES

The fact that the vast majority of Americans in 1998 were not presented with a competitive House race is worrisome. Electoral competition is an important mechanism for promoting the accountability and responsibility of political leaders to the people. House incumbents who face no serious challenge cannot be removed from office. Their constituents have no direct electoral means of expressing dissatisfaction with their performance in office. Indeed, without a vigorous campaign mounted by a skilled opponent, many constituents lack the information necessary to assess their representative's performance and come to a reasoned judgment about whether the incumbent should continue in office. In short, electoral competition is the lifeblood of democracy. Our democracy is based on the judgments of citizens in locally defined geographic areas. While the contest over partisan control of the institution is an extremely important form of electoral competition, the lack of meaningful contests in many House districts is a very troublesome aspect of contemporary American politics.

Our premise is that if higher-quality candidates ran for the House, the average district race would be more competitive. In the case of the districts in which there was no major-party challenger to the incumbent, this is clearly true. However, in many of the districts in which incumbents faced a challenger from the opposite party, we also believe that had stronger candidates run, the races would have been more competitive.

To be sure, many political factors, such as the partisan makeup of the district, local and national economic conditions, political scandals, and even competition among candidates for other offices, affect the success even of high-quality candidates and the competitiveness of House races. Moreover, because many high-quality individuals act strategically in selecting when to run, not only will political conditions affect their chances of success, but these same conditions are also likely to affect their choice of whether or not to enter the race. Thus, political conditions and candidate quality often interact with one another to limit or enhance the choices citizens have in U.S. House elections.

Nonetheless, other things being equal, a high-quality challenger can make a race against an entrenched incumbent more competitive than can a challenger of lesser quality. Given this premise, it is important to assess the supply of high-quality candidates nationwide and to understand what motivates those who are of high quality to enter the race for a House seat. In this chapter, we contend that a significant number of high-quality potential candidates can be identified in every House district, including those that have not been competitive in the past. However, most potential candidates choose not to run for office, thereby reducing the level of competition in the typical House campaign by some undetermined, but significant, amount.

To explore the availability and choice of high-quality potential candidates for the House, we must first have a good working definition of candidate "quality." We must also have a way of identifying high-quality candidates who decide not to run if we are to understand the decision process that leads many to opt out of running for Congress. Once high-quality potential candidates are identified, we can explore some of the reasons they choose not to run in order to consider the factors that might induce stronger candidates to enter the fray. The next section of this chapter addresses the definition and measurement of candidate quality. In this section we define two key dimensions of candidate quality and demonstrate that we can identify a broad range of individuals of high quality who are strong *potential* candidates for office. In the second section, we explore some of the many reasons the potential candidates identified by the study did not become *actual* candidates for a seat in the U.S. House.

WHAT IS A HIGH-QUALITY CANDIDATE?

In the strictest sense, most citizens can be considered potential candidates for the U.S. House because the legal qualifications to run for office are minimal. Any U.S. citizen who is 25 years of age or older and resides in a state for some specified length of time is eligible to run.[1] However, while they may be well-liked and respected within their community, the average bank teller, contractor, grocer, or accountant is unlikely to mount a credible challenge to a House incumbent because they are not well-known and because, in all likelihood, they have not developed the political capital necessary to run a viable campaign. Instead, when we think of high-quality candidates, we tend to think of individuals who are not only respected in their communities, but who are also well-known and who clearly possess some necessary political resources. Perhaps they hold state or local political offices. Or perhaps they are prominent business, religious, or community leaders. Or perhaps they have demonstrated an ability and willingness to spend a good deal of money on politics. At any rate, the individuals who come to mind generally have some quality or set of qualities that make them stronger potential candidates than the average citizen who meets the minimum requirements. The question is, what are the traits that lead some citizens to be viewed as "high-quality" candidates or more "qualified" to run for office than others?

We define a high-quality candidate as one who has the skills and resources necessary to run a competitive campaign. That is to say, because our concern is to identify potential candidates who have the ability to provide citizens with a meaningful choice through competitive, visible campaigns, the definition of quality we use captures the resources and skills that candidates must possess in order to ensure their ability to run a visible campaign that would be attractive to citizens in their districts.

What sorts of skills and resources are we talking about? We think of candidate quality as composed of two dimensions: *strategic* resources that bear directly on an individual's ability to mount a successful campaign, and *personal* characteristics that are important both in the campaign and as an officeholder.[2]

The strategic resources or abilities a candidate brings to a race are an important part of a potential candidate's quality. After all, campaigns are fundamentally exercises in visibility, mobilization, and persuasion. Candidates who have the tools at their disposal to help them generate high levels of positive publicity, and who can persuade others to support their efforts to win office, are likely to be more successful in their efforts. Candidates must possess a cluster of skills that enable them to mobilize key supporters, such as political party leaders, community leaders, or interest groups and persuade political actors of the value of their cause. Those who can do so are in a better position to mount a competitive campaign and garner positive attention from voters.

More and more, contemporary campaigns depend on large amounts of money, and therefore much of the success of a campaign depends on candidates' ability to persuade contributors to support them. In fact, scholars estimate that the average price tag for beating an incumbent House member rose from $400,000 in 1992 to just over $1,000,000 in 1996.[3] Thus, a candidate's ability to gain the support of contributors is of paramount importance in successfully challenging an incumbent. Of course, it can also be a tremendous advantage to command enough personal wealth to fund one's own campaign.

Strategic qualities are not the only qualities voters or political supporters look for in candidates. Ask an average citizen what kind of candidate she would like to see run in the next House election, and she will be unlikely to say, "I'd like to see a good fund-raiser run this time." She would also be unlikely to mention that she wants someone to run who has a high level of name recognition in the district. She is much more likely to say she would like to see candidates of high integrity, who can be effective legislators and who are committed to public service. As political scientists who have studied many campaigns and thought seriously about how democratic politics should work, we agree. Candidate quality means more than the sheer ability to get elected. It implies something about the personal qualities we all would like to see in those representing our side in an election campaign, and it implies something about the qualities we want to see in those who hold office.

Nevertheless, the average citizen would probably agree that it would not do much good to find someone of great personal integrity, who could get lots of good things done in office, and who is dedicated to serving the public, if that person lacked the strategic skills and resources to get elected. In other words, the best candidate is one who has both desirable leadership qualities *and* the ability to run an effective campaign. So personal qualities, while important, are not enough. But neither is the sheer ability to get elected. Both dimensions of candidate quality are important to a common-sense understanding of the concept.

Because of the importance of understanding candidate quality and its relationship to the competitiveness of House elections, we felt it was necessary to reexamine the question with a broader concept of quality to encompass both the personal and strategic aspects of quality. Other scholars have tended to emphasize the "strategic" or "electability" side in their discussions of candidate quality. We are sympathetic with this view because it is consistent with the importance we attach to competitiveness in elections. However, this approach does not fully account for personal qualities, which bear directly on candidates' abilities to be good leaders. Certainly, the fact that a potential candidate has an array of strategic advantages may imply that the candidate has strong personal qualities as well, given that it is likely that political supporters are attracted to candidates with such personal qualities. While we are comfortable thinking that those with strategic qualities have strong personal qualities, we cannot be sure without more precise measures of each of these concepts.

Expanding the definition of candidate quality beyond that normally used by political commentators and political scientists can also help to identify differences in the qualities among those currently holding office and to provide a means of assessing the strength of individuals who have never held elective office. The most frequently used measure of candidate quality has been whether or not the individual has officeholding experience.[4] Indeed, this measure has served scholars well in exploring the role of challengers in enhancing electoral competitiveness. For example, Jacobson and Kernell showed that candidates who had previously held elected office consistently fared better in elections than those without such experience.[5] Nevertheless, we argue that a measure of officeholding experience fails to capture important dimensions of potential candidate quality. To be sure, experience in elected office makes sense as a measure of the strategic side of candidate quality, because office-holders have demonstrated the ability to win an election; the ability to win one office relates to the ability to win another. Officeholding experience also makes sense as a measure because it is readily ascertainable from documentary sources and it is logically prior to the candidate's actual performance in the House election. However, officeholding directly measures only the strategic side of candidate quality. Moreover, it is silent about *which* strategic resources and qualities are most important in helping candidates win elections.

Additionally, measuring candidate quality through previous electoral experience is problematic because electoral experience is clearly a variable that should hold different weight under different circumstances. A town councilor who might represent 5,000 or 10,000 citizens and a state senator who might represent hundreds of thousands of citizens are not equal in their experience or in their ability to mount a campaign for a U.S. House seat, even though both have successfully won elective office.[6] Even candidates of identical office rank may have diverse skills. For example, the fund-raising skill of a state legislator from California, where the average campaign expenditure for a seat exceeds $300,000, is likely to be very different from the fund-raising skill of a state legislator from Wyoming, where the average expenditure is just over $4,000.[7] Furthermore, the measure fails to distinguish quality among non-officeholders who might seek office. We know that many non-officeholders have won seats in Congress in recent elections. Measures of quality that rely solely on previous experience ignore this important group of candidates altogether.

To explore the decision process of potential candidates fully, we need measures of quality that describe a prospective candidate's strategic abilities and personal characteristics before he or she decides to run so that the measures can be applied to those who choose not to run. In addition, we need measures to assess the quality of individuals who have never held elective office because an increasing number of competitive candidates are drawn from careers outside of politics. Only by identifying quality separate from officeholding and prior to the campaign can we use the measures to compare the qualities of potential candidates with the qualities of those who actually run or already hold public office.

ASSESSING THE QUALITY OF POTENTIAL CANDIDATES

We undertook the Candidate Emergence Study to research the decision-making process of potential candidates in 200 randomly selected House districts across the country. Indeed, a major concern was that many high-quality potential U.S. House candidates decide *not* to run. In this study, we surveyed politically knowledgeable "informants" in each of our sampled districts to identify and learn about high-quality potential candidates in their area. We also asked them for assessments of the incumbents in their districts. As a second stage in our research, we surveyed the potential candidates recommended by our informants and state legislators whose districts overlapped with our sample of congressional districts to learn more about the many factors that might influence their desire to run for a House seat. The data on which this chapter is based comes from those two surveys. The Candidate Emergence Study is discussed in greater detail in the appendix to this chapter.

The first question of interest is whether informants were able to identify a broad pool of individuals who possess the qualities we believe are related to candidates' abilities to run competitive campaigns. We begin with our informants' quality ratings of the individuals whom they named as strong potential candidates in their House district. We asked informants to rate potential candidates in response to a variety of questions designed to tap the two dimensions of candidate quality: strategic qualities and resources, and personal qualities. We also asked informants to rate the incumbent representative in their district on many of the same items. These responses give us a way of directly assessing the quality of potential candidates and provide a way to compare their quality with the quality of incumbents. Because there is a tendency for informants' partisanship to bias their perceptions, all informant ratings throughout this chapter have been statistically adjusted to remove the effects of partisan perceptual bias.[8]

In Table 2-1, note first that informants rated both potential candidates and incumbents very highly on the items we used to measure the two quality dimensions. The overwhelming majority of informants rated potential candidates and incumbents as "strong" on the 7-point scales we asked them to use in their ratings.[9] The high ratings suggest first of all that informants followed our instructions in naming strong potential candidates, and secondly that they have a great deal of respect for incumbent representatives in their district.

POTENTIAL CANDIDATE QUALITY

Overwhelmingly, informants rated their potential candidates as having one or more strengths in the areas of strategic resources, personal qualities, or both. In fact, in only 8 of 2,325 informant assessments were potential candidates rated as fair or weak on all quality items listed in Table 2-1. Thus, nearly all potential candidates were recommended for one or more strong qualities on the dimensions of interest. However, not all candidates were rated strong on all items, leading to the variation shown in the table.

Two-thirds of potential candidates were seen as having strong name recognition in the district, indicating that many of the recommended individuals hold high-profile positions of one sort or another in their communities. A full three-quarters were rated as having strong fund-raising abilities.

TABLE 2-1 INFORMANT ASSESSMENTS OF POTENTIAL CANDIDATES' AND INCUMBENTS'
STRATEGIC AND PERSONAL QUALITIES (% RATED "STRONG")

	POTENTIAL CANDIDATES	INCUMBENTS	POTENTIAL CANDIDATES RATED *HIGHER* THAN INCUMBENT
Strategic Qualities			
Name recognition	66	90	17
Ability to raise money to fund campaign	75	93	16
Support from political party	72	84	28
Support from interest groups outside the district	83	NA	NA
Ability to fund own campaign	38	NA	NA
Strategic Quality Index	75	94	17
Personal Qualities			
Integrity	83	78	36
Ability to find solutions to problems	72	63	45
Ability to work with other political leaders	72	73	35
Public speaking abilities	83	73	53
Dedication to serving the public	91	79	58
Grasp of the issues	82	79	35
Personal Quality Index	85	73	42
Overall Assessment of Strength	80	86	26
Smallest number of cases	*1,988*	*1,314*	*1,889*

Source: Candidate Emergence Study, Informant Survey.

As mentioned earlier, fund-raising ability has become an increasingly important aspect of mounting a competitive campaign. The fact that informants see so many of these candidates as strong in this area attests to the strength of this pool of individuals. Additionally, many potential candidates were expected to have strong support from their political party and from interest groups outside the district. Certainly, these findings mirror the accepted understanding of the importance of strategic resources in contemporary campaigns.

It is interesting to note, however, that the most widespread strong qualities of potential candidates are the *personal* qualities. Informants, in large part, identified individuals whom they believe had strong leadership qualities such as dedication to public service, integrity, a strong grasp of the issues, and the ability to communicate well. It appears that the individuals who come to mind as potential candidates have many of the types of qualities the public seeks in public officials. These findings reinforce our view that personal quality plays an important role in making individuals attractive as candidates to political activists as well as to voters.

Notice that by far the lowest rating is for potential candidates' ability to fund their own campaign, with only 38 percent of informants rating their potential candidates as strong in this regard.[10] This is clear evidence that our informants do not regard personal wealth as the *sine qua non* of a strong potential House challenger, given that the majority of the individuals they named are not able to fund their own House campaigns. It is perhaps reassuring that other qualities besides personal wealth were evidently uppermost in informants' minds as they considered who in their district might make a strong House contender.[11]

COMPARING POTENTIAL CANDIDATES AND INCUMBENTS

Despite the generally positive quality ratings of potential candidates, there are important differences in the results, especially when we compare the strength of potential candidates to the strength of incumbents. By far most incumbents are consistently rated as stronger on the strategic qualities that we asked about. In their name recognition, in their ability to raise money to fund their campaign, and in their support from their political party outside the district, incumbents have a substantial edge over potential candidates who might challenge them. These strategic advantages of incumbents are reflected in the summary Strategic Quality Index that combines the items used in common for incumbents and potential candidates. On that measure, virtually all informants rate incumbents on the strong side, as compared with three-quarters who rate potential candidates as strong. Moreover, in a direct comparison, only 17 percent of potential candidates were rated as stronger than the incumbent on this index. Because strategic qualities figure very prominently in any candidate's electoral success, the advantage that incumbents enjoy over the strongest of their potential challengers is striking.

The advantages that incumbents enjoy in strategic quality evaporates when we consider the personal qualities of potential candidates and incumbents. While many incumbents are rated highly on such qualities as integrity, their ability to find solutions to problems, and their dedication to serving the public, potential candidates are rated even more positively. A large number of potential candidates are rated *higher* than incumbents. In fact, well over half of potential candidates are rated as having stronger dedication to serving the public than the incumbent, and nearly half are believed to have a stronger ability to find solutions to problems.

On the Personal Quality Index, potential candidates end up with a substantial edge over incumbents, as fully 85 percent receive strong ratings, compared with 73 percent of incumbents. Indeed, 42 percent of potential candidates ranked higher than the incumbent in their district on this important dimension of quality. In fairness to incumbents, we must recognize that informants' ratings of potential candidates were of individuals whom they had selected, whereas their incumbent ratings were of individuals whom they would not necessarily have singled out as strong. Nevertheless, it seems reasonable to conclude that on personal qualities, potential candidates are at least the equal of incumbents, whereas on strategic qualities, incumbents generally enjoy a substantial advantage. When asked to provide an overall general rating of potential candidates and incumbents (the last item in Table 2-1), the advantage incumbents have on the strategic side apparently tips the ratings in their favor. Only a scant 26 percent of potential candidates rated higher than incumbents on the measure of overall strength as candidates.

POTENTIAL CANDIDATE QUALITY AND THE CHANCE OF WINNING

The question of incumbency advantage is an important one we will return to in the second section of this chapter. For now, our focus remains on assessing the quality of the potential candidates named by our informants. Since the central task of the first phase of the Candidate Emergence Study was to identify a pool of individuals with qualities that might affect the competitiveness of congressional races should they choose to run, we need to know whether the various qualities outlined in Table 2-1 are related to the chances a candidate could win. Can we find evidence that the quality of potential candidates affects their chances of winning?

Table 2-2 (on page 22) and Figure 2-1 (on page 23) suggest that the answer is yes. Table 2-2 shows that informants consistently judge potential candidates whom they see to be higher in quality also to be higher in their chances of winning.[12] This table indicates that potential candidates who were rated higher on strategic characteristics were seen as much more likely to win a House seat if they had chosen to run. Indeed, potential candidates rated as strong on the overall Strategic Quality Index were expected to have a nearly 1 in 3 chance of winning, while those judged to be fair or weak were expected to have only a 1 in 6 chance. In other words, strategic strengths doubled the average chance of winning.

While the differences are especially sharp on strategic qualities, they are also consistently present for personal qualities. It is reassuring to know that, at least in the minds of informants, higher personal qualities are associated with a greater chance of winning a House seat. While the differences on personal qualities are not as dramatic as they are for the strategic items, this table clearly demonstrates that such qualities represent an important dimension of strength for potential candidates. Moreover, the cumulative effect of personal quality, as measured by the Personal Quality Index, shows the substantial effect of a combination of these qualities.

Figure 2-1 explores the direct effect of the strategic and personal quality indices on potential candidate chances. As we found in looking at the individual

TABLE 2-2   CANDIDATE QUALITY AND OVERALL
PROBABILITY OF WINNING—INFORMANT ASSESSMENTS

	QUALITY RATED AT LEAST "SOMEWHAT STRONG"[a]	QUALITY RATED AS "FAIR" OR "WEAK"[b]	DIFFERENCE OF MEAN CHANCE OF WINNING
Strategic Qualities			
Name recognition	.32	.16	.16*
Support from political party	.31	.18	.13*
Ability to raise money to fund campaign	.30	.15	.15*
Ability to fund own campaign	.33	.23	.10*
Support from interest groups outside the district	.29	.15	.14*
Strategic Quality Index	.31	.15	.16*
Personal Qualities			
Integrity	.28	.19	.09*
Ability to find solutions to problems	.30	.19	.11*
Ability to work with other political leaders	.30	.19	.11*
Public speaking abilities	.28	.21	.07*
Dedication to serving the public	.27	.18	.09*
Grasp of the issues	.29	.18	.11*
Personal Quality Index	.29	.16	.13*
Overall Quality of Potential Candidate	.30	.12	.18*
Smallest number of cases			*1,777*

[a]Informant rated the candidate as "somewhat strong," "strong," or "extremely strong" for the listed quality.
[b]Informant rated the potential candidate as "fair," "somewhat weak," "weak," or "extremely weak" for the listed quality.
*Difference of means is statistically significant at $p|t| < .001$.

items, strategic qualities appear to have a stronger direct effect on potential candidate chances than personal qualities. Does this mean that personal qualities aren't important? Not at all. Indeed, the simple fact that so many of the potential candidates named by the informants have strong personal qualities shows the relevance of these qualities in political leaders' thinking about who would be a strong candidate. Moreover, personal qualities appear to have an indirect effect on potential candidate chances through their influence on strategic qualities. That is, other things being equal, a candidate's ability to raise money or attract support of other kinds will be enhanced if he or she is recognized as having high integrity, a good grasp of the issues, the ability to work with other political leaders, and so on.[13]

FIGURE 2-1   POTENTIAL CANDIDATES' CHANCES OF WINNING

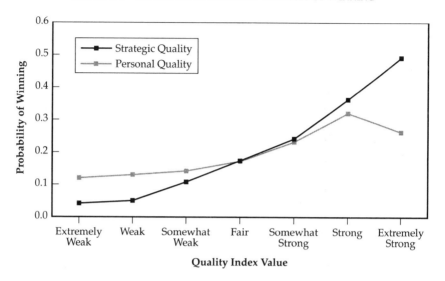

THE AVAILABILITY OF QUALITY CANDIDATES

Having established that there are, indeed, a large number of qualified candidates for office, we turn now to the question of whether high-quality potential candidates are available in all House districts, including those thought to be noncompetitive. In other words, one possible explanation for the lack of strong potential candidates in many U.S. House districts is that there simply is an undersupply of such individuals, especially in districts where no strong candidate runs.

Table 2-3 (on page 24) examines this question directly by looking at the availability of quality candidates in districts with different levels of competitiveness. We compare the supply of high-quality potential candidates in the party opposite the incumbent with the supply of such potential candidates in the incumbent's party in each of the different district contexts.[14] It is clear that our informants were able to identify strong potential candidates even in districts that were completely noncompetitive in 1998.[15] Informants identified, on average, 10 strong potential candidates in each district. Even our informants from less competitive districts—including those in which no major party candidate challenged an incumbent—were able to identify many individuals in their districts who met their criteria as high-quality candidates. Potential candidates were identified both in the party of the incumbent and in the other party, in districts that exhibited all levels of competition.

Not only do such potential candidates exist, but they are indeed very high-quality candidates. For example, fully 87 percent of the potential candidates

TABLE 2-3   QUALITY OF POTENTIAL CANDIDATES (PCs)
BY DISTRICT COMPETITION AND PARTY

	INCUMBENT HAD NO MAJOR PARTY CHALLENGER IN 1998		1998 HOUSE RACE WAS NOT COMPETITIVE[a]		1998 HOUSE RACE WAS COMPETITIVE[b]	
Number of districts in study[c]	39		105		48	
Average number of PCs per district	10		10		10	
	IN-PARTY PCs	OUT-PARTY PCs	IN-PARTY PCs	OUT-PARTY PCs	IN-PARTY PCs	OUT-PARTY PCs
Average number of PCs identified per district	5	4	4	5	4	6
Rated strong on Strategic Quality Index	71%	69%	77%	66%	72%	69%
Rated strong on Personal Quality Index	80%	87%	87%	85%	87%	86%
Smallest number of cases	187	158	435	513	183	281

[a]The major party challenger received less than 40% of the vote in the district.
[b]The major party challenger received 40% or more of the vote in the district.
[c]Informants provided names of PCs in 192 of the 200 districts included in the Study.

identified by informants *in districts where no candidate in that party emerged to run against the incumbent* were rated as strong on the Personal Quality Index. In fact, while the percentage of potential candidates rated strong on the Personal Qualities Index is high in all types of districts, it is actually highest among out-party potential candidates in districts where no one in the party ran! While the ratings on strategic qualities are not quite as high as ratings on personal qualities, for all districts that witnessed all levels of competition in 1998, they remain impressively high.

SUMMARY

Taken together, the tables from this section present compelling evidence that many high-quality challengers are available, some of whom rate even higher than incumbents on some aspects of candidate quality. As a first attempt to provide in-depth systematic quality ratings of potential candidates for the House that go beyond their officeholding experience, the data yield important insights into the quality and availability of potential challengers.[16] While incumbents enjoy a clear advantage in strategic quality, they are at least matched, if not exceeded, in personal quality by their strongest potential challengers in their districts. Incumbency carries inherent strategic resource advantages that are impossible for most challengers to match, but these advantages are rather narrowly limited to those directly bearing on electoral prospects—name recognition or visibility in the district, fund-raising ability, and the like. On the sorts of qualities that most people want to see in their representatives (and in candidates running in their districts), there appears to be no lack of high-quality potential candidates.

The data are reassuring if the question is whether a pool of potential candidates that has the personal qualities most of us would like to see in candidates and officeholders exists in most districts. The results are somewhat more troubling when we recognize the strategic advantages that incumbents have over their strongest potential challengers and consider how such advantages may influence the choice of these high-quality citizens to run for office.

THE CHOICE TO RUN: WHY POTENTIAL CANDIDATES OPT OUT

The responses of informants across the districts included in the study show the presence of individuals who were well qualified to run for the U.S. House in 1998. However, only a small number of districts had truly competitive challengers. Why should this be the case? If so many qualified individuals exist, why did they not run?

In this section, we explore why the existence of high-quality potential candidates did not translate into more competitive races. The short answer is that most of these qualified potential candidates chose not to run. The mere existence of high-quality candidates is not enough. These individuals must have the requisite amount of political ambition to consider a run for office. They must have an interest in the House of Representatives as a body in which they would like to serve. Those with that ambition and interest must then make the ultimate decision to enter the race for a seat in the House in a particular election year. The existence of a pool of qualified candidates is a necessary condition to increase the competitiveness of House elections, but it is not a *sufficient* condition. At the very least, these candidates must take the steps from potential candidate to actual candidate.

One of the advantages of the two-stage design of the Candidate Emergence Study is that we can explore these types of "supply-side" questions through analyzing survey responses from the potential candidates themselves. Table 2-4 provides an overview of the characteristics of the potential candidates who responded to the second-stage survey. Just over half of the respondents meet the commonly used scholarly standard for "quality," in that they hold elective office. Nearly half, 44 percent, of respondents come from other professional backgrounds and would have been missed using traditional measures to identify quality potential candidates. Notably, nearly all respondents rank highly on one or both of the quality indices created from the informant responses. Thus, our pool of respondents is precisely the type we are interested in studying— respondents who are of high quality, either strategically, personally, or both.

TABLE 2-4   CHARACTERISTICS OF RESPONDENTS
TO THE POTENTIAL CANDIDATE (PC) SURVEY*

	% OF ALL RESPONDENTS
Political Experience	
State legislator	30
Holds elective office, other than state legislator	26
Holds appointive office	13
Quality	
Informants view PC as "somewhat strong" or stronger on:	
Personal Quality Index	89
Strategic Quality Index	67
Ambition	
Interested in or open to holding elective office in future	90
Attracted to career in the U.S. House	70
Plan to Run for U.S. House Seat	
In the foreseeable future	43
In 1998	6
Smallest number of cases	*395*

*Includes only informant-recommended potential candidates.

Of greater importance, however, is the political ambition held by these potential candidates. Table 2-4 shows that many of these individuals harbor ambitions to hold political office, including a U.S. House seat. A scant 10 percent of respondents felt no interest in seeking or holding elective office. Moreover, a full 70 percent of the respondents indicated that they were attracted to a career in the House.

However, big steps separate having political ambition and interest from actually planning to run. Fewer than half of the respondents believe they are likely to run in some future election, and only 6 percent thought it likely they would run in 1998. This disconnect presents a most important puzzle for political scientists and for those interested in the health of American democracy: If there are high-quality individuals who are politically ambitious and attracted to a career in the House, why don't they run?

POTENTIAL CANDIDATES' CHANCES OF WINNING

One explanation for why potential candidates do not run has been hinted at throughout the chapter: Many potential candidates do not believe they can win. We saw in Table 2-1, for example, that incumbent House members enjoy substantial advantages over potential candidates in the strategic qualities that enhance a candidate's ability to win. Indeed, as Table 2-2 showed, even potential candidates who were rated strong on strategic qualities were still estimated to have only a 1 in 3 chance of winning. If potential candidates see the world in much the same way informants do, they may feel very discouraged at the prospect of entering a race that they are unlikely to win.

How, then, do potential candidates view their electoral prospects? We can answer this by looking at the responses potential candidates gave to a series of questions asking about their expected chances of winning should they choose to run for a House seat.[17] Table 2-5 presents the average probability of winning each stage of the nomination as well as the joint probability of winning the seat.

The results presented in Table 2-5 suggest that, as suspected, potential candidates see incumbents as a formidable hurdle. Clearly, potential candidates

TABLE 2-5   POTENTIAL CANDIDATE (PC) CHANCES OF WINNING
IN 1998, BY WHETHER SEAT WAS OPEN IN 1998

	OPEN SEAT IN 1998	INCUMBENT RAN IN 1998
PC chances of winning primary if runs	.52	.42
PC chances of winning general election if wins primary	.55	.43
PC chances of winning seat	.34	.18
Smallest number of cases	23	362

believed their chances of winning to be substantially higher in open seats than they were in districts where the incumbent was running. This was true of their chances in both the nomination and general election stages, and especially of their overall chances of winning the seat, if they decided to enter the race. Indeed, their chances of winning the seat were judged as almost twice as high in districts where no incumbent would be running as in districts where a prospective candidate would have to defeat an incumbent in either the nomination or the general election in order to win the seat. The reason the effect is greater on winning the seat is because that estimate of chances is the result of multiplying each potential candidate's perceived chances of winning the nomination by his or her chances of winning the general election. This multiplicative effect magnifies the relative differences evident in each stage, amounting to a dramatic difference in chances of winning the seat linked to the presence or absence of an incumbent.

At the same time, Table 2-5 masks important differences in each stage, depending on whether the potential candidate and the incumbent are in the same political party. Table 2-6 shows that when the potential candidate and the incumbent are in the same party, potential candidates judge their chances of winning the nomination as much lower than when the potential candidate and incumbent are in the opposite party. This makes perfect sense. Potential candidates in the incumbent's party must contemplate beating an individual who has a substantial advantage in strategic resources.

Out-party potential candidates, by definition, do not face an incumbent in the nomination phase. Not surprisingly, the chances that a high-quality challenger will win a nomination race are quite high in comparison with the prospects of the in-party potential candidate.[18]

The situation is reversed in the general election stage. In-party potential candidates have better than twice the chance of winning the election as out-party potential candidates. Potential candidates in the party opposite the incumbent must anticipate running their general election campaign against an

TABLE 2-6   POTENTIAL CANDIDATES' PERCEIVED CHANCES OF WINNING
BY WHETHER THEY ARE IN THE SAME PARTY AS THE INCUMBENT

	INCUMBENT RAN IN 1998	
	PC AND INCUMBENT IN SAME PARTY	*PC AND INCUMBENT IN OPPOSITE PARTIES*
PC chances of winning primary if runs	.18	.62
PC chances of winning general election if wins primary	.60	.28
PC chances of winning seat	.13	.22
Smallest number of cases	*167*	*194*

incumbent—a prospect only slightly more inviting than challenging a sitting representative for his or her party's nomination.[19] In-party potential candidates answered the question about their chances of winning the general election *if* they had their party's nomination, so by definition, they would not be facing an incumbent in the fall election.

In fact their improved chances are due to the twin effects of *not* facing an incumbent at that stage, and of the fact that most of them share the party identification of the dominant party in the district. Because many districts are dominated by one party and tend to elect incumbents from that party, many in-party potential candidates would have the advantage of running in a district where the partisan predisposition of their district worked to their advantage. Thus, when potential candidates assess their chances of winning, they appear to do so with an eye both to the incumbent and to the partisan makeup of the district.[20]

The results from Table 2-5 confirm that potential candidates see their chances of beating an incumbent as extremely low. Potential candidates who would have to unseat an incumbent to get into the House estimated their chances of winning as less than 1 in 5. Even in open seats, potential candidates gave themselves only about a 1 in 3 chance of winning, if they were to decide to run.

Given such low odds of winning in 1998, it can hardly be surprising to learn that chances of winning have a direct bearing on the decision to run.[21] The vast majority of these individuals chose not to gamble their current positions, be they political or private, on a risky run for the House. Incumbents have access to so many resources to help them retain their seats—free postage privileges, the ability to provide constituent services, the ability to gain strong financial backing from interest groups and political parties—that many potential candidates see little chance of competing seriously, much less of winning. Thus many potential candidates quit before they ever start.

The data in Table 2-7 illustrate how the chances of winning and the prospect of facing an incumbent impact the choice to run. Potential candidates in open seats and/or in districts where they judged their chances of winning to be better than 50-50 were substantially more likely to think seriously about running in 1998 than potential candidates whose opportunity to win was lower. Indeed, potential candidates named by our informants were

TABLE 2-7   POTENTIAL CANDIDATES' CHANCES OF RUNNING IN 1998

	SEAT OPEN IN 1998?		PERCEIVED CHANCES OF WINNING THE SEAT	
	No	YES	≤ .49	≥ .50
Percent likely to run in 1998	5%	25%	4%	26%
Number of cases	382	24	337	38

five times more likely to seriously consider running in open seats than in districts where an incumbent was running for reelection.

Evidence of this phenomenon is readily apparent in news accounts of challengers who emerge to run for seats vacated by incumbents. For example, newspapers report numerous strong candidates entering the arena in 2000 to run for retiring Nebraska Republican Bill Barrett's seat in the House. The race has drawn such notables as Tom Osborne, the well-known retired football coach from the University of Nebraska, along with a former chair of the Republican state party, the former state chair of the Christian Coalition, and two statewide officeholders.[22] Yet only two years ago, Representative Barrett ran unchallenged in both the primary and general elections. Not a single candidate was willing to enter a contest against the popular incumbent. When the incumbent Barrett was no longer an obstacle, however, many high-quality potential candidates who had stayed in the background before were now willing to compete for the office.

However, even where an incumbent is not running, we may still find that candidate entry in the district remains lopsided in favoring one party more than the other. This stems from the fact that many districts still lean heavily in one partisan direction or the other, and the party favored is typically the party of the previous incumbent. Thus, potential candidates in the same party as the incumbent see the nomination as especially valuable because the chances that it will lead to election are greater than would be the case if the other party were dominant. As a result, more "in-party" potential candidates are likely to run, and competition for the nomination will be more difficult. In contrast, competition for the general election would be less strenuous, and the chances of winning that election, assuming the nomination was won, would be greater. For potential candidates not in the party of the previous incumbent, the opposite situations prevail. The nomination would be seen as less valuable (because it was less likely to lead to a general election victory), thus fewer high-quality potential candidates would be likely to seek it. Therefore, each individual potential candidate's chances of winning the nomination would be greater. Conversely, the chances of winning the general election would be smaller because of the partisan predilection of the district for the other party.

In this light, it is not surprising to discover that the vast majority, though not all, of the high-quality candidates seeking Nebraska's district 3 seat are in the Republican Party. District 3 is heavily Republican; that partisan advantage contributed to Barrett's seeming invulnerability, just as did his incumbency. With the incumbent removed from the election calculus, the GOP partisan advantage still leads those considering the race to conclude that the Republican nominee is virtually assured of a general election victory. Thus, while the open seat drew a number of high-quality Republican candidates, it drew only a single Democratic candidate into the race. This example goes far toward reinforcing our understanding that there are many forces that shape the contours of competition in House districts aside from candidate quality.

Certainly the fact that these long-time residents of district 3 chose to wait for an open seat hints at how potential candidates wait for a strategic opportunity to run—that is, they run when their expected chance of winning is highest. Indeed, Table 2-7 demonstrates a direct link between chances of winning and chances of running. Potential candidates were more than six times more likely to run in 1998 if they saw their chances of winning as at least a tossup, compared with potential candidates who saw their chances of winning as low. To sum up very simply, one very important part of the explanation for why strong potential candidates do not run is that despite their strength, they do not think they can win.[23]

OTHER FACTORS THAT DISCOURAGE POTENTIAL CANDIDATES FROM RUNNING

But there is more to the explanation of why potential candidates do not run than assessments of their chances. Representative Martin Frost (D-TX, former Democratic Congressional Campaign Committee chair) pointed to the importance of this sort of strategic calculation that potential candidates must make, while also acknowledging the enormous commitment that is required to mount a successful House campaign:

> First, they [potential candidates] can't raise the money necessary. Second, they are unwilling to take a year or a year and a half out of their lives. And third—and this is different from 20 or 30 years ago—even those who think they can win are not sure they want to do it.... When I first ran, this job was really considered a plum for everyone. It is not so now.[24]

Similar themes were sounded by two potential candidates recently interviewed by Robin Toner of the *New York Times*, both of whom decided against running in the 2000 elections.[25] Florida state representative Lori Edwards thought at first that her campaign might cost under half a million dollars, but she soon learned that the real price tag was closer to $1 million. That might not have deterred her except that if she won, she "would have to turn around and raise $1 million again" to seek reelection in a district that might not be redrawn to her benefit after the 2000 census. Her colleague in the statehouse, Republican Adam Putnam, worried not so much about the cost of the campaign as about the fact that much of the money would come from out of state and would consist of independent expenditures out of his control. "[T]hat message is going to be what these out-of-towners are going to be saying about you and on your behalf.... That's spooky to me."[26]

In his experience recruiting and working with candidates, Congressman Frost saw many who were deterred by the difficulty of balancing family life and political ambitions:

In some instances [potential candidates choose not to run] because of young families, wives who don't want to move to DC. Young fathers don't want to be away from their children when they are growing up. That really is a major factor these days. Also wives with careers that they don't want to abandon.[27]

Frost's words were echoed nearly verbatim by another of Toner's interviewees, Rick Dantzler, a 43-year-old Florida Democrat whom party leaders were encouraging to run for Congress: "I'm sure the kids will be fine.… And I am sure that [my wife] Julie and I will stay together. But I am not sure that I want to miss [that time with my kids]."[28]

Many close observers have argued that the process of campaigning and serving in public office may be an increasingly strong deterrent to highly qualified candidates. Candidates seeking a House seat may need to raise a million dollars or more just to run a credible campaign. The campaign season starts early, as candidates must begin raising money far in advance of the primary in their quest for their party's nomination. The enormous amount of time needed for campaigning, the constant media scrutiny, and negative campaign tactics take their toll on candidates and their families.

Responses to our potential candidate survey indicate that such concerns are well founded. The vast majority of potential candidates are discouraged by one or more aspects of the process involved in running for and holding a House seat (see Table 2-8). The two most widely cited factors discouraging potential candidates were the need to raise large amounts of money and

TABLE 2-8   FACTORS DISCOURAGING POTENTIAL CANDIDATES
FROM RUNNING FOR THE U.S. HOUSE (%)

	AT LEAST SOMEWHAT DISCOURAGED[a]
Personal Concerns	
Loss of personal and family privacy	66
Enduring negative advertising attacks	64
Separation from family and friends	83
Loss of leisure time	53
Monetary and Career Concerns	
Have to raise large amounts of money	86
Lack of assistance from political party	67
Possibility of serving in minority party in Congress	26
Impact on political career if runs and loses	32
Have to give up current career	46
Smallest number of cases	*428*

[a]The question reads: "Please indicate how the following factors would influence your interest in running for the U.S. House." Potential candidates could respond "make no difference," "somewhat discourage," "discourage," or "strongly discourage," to each listed survey item. This column gives the percentage of all respondents who answered in one of the latter three categories.

separation from family and friends. Surprisingly, career concerns proved discouraging to far fewer potential candidates. The majority were unconcerned about the impact losing would have on their political career, although close to half expressed reservations about having to give up their current career in order to run and serve in Congress.

Personal concerns weighed heavily in the responses of our potential candidates. In addition to the very large proportion worried about separation from family and friends, two-thirds were discouraged by the lack of privacy that accompanies today's media-saturated campaigns and service in high public office. Sixty-four percent were discouraged by the prospect of enduring negative advertising in a campaign, and 53 percent worried about giving up control over their leisure time should they win office. These findings demonstrate that the profound changes in personal lifestyle that result from entering a campaign loom large in the minds of many potential candidates, and affect the likelihood that they will seek office.

CONCLUSION

A healthy democracy depends on competitive elections, and the lack of competition in contemporary U.S. House elections is worrisome.[29] While we recognize that many factors influence the competitiveness of House races, the quality of the candidates who decide to run is certainly important. To investigate this question, we must be able to study a non-event: the strong potential candidate who decides not to run. Our desire to study this question motivated us to grapple with a more complete definition of the "quality" of candidates and to find a way to identify individuals who would make strong candidates even though they might decide against running for public office.

What have we learned? The availability of potential candidates with serious ambition to run for the House is not the problem. Plenty of potential candidates can be found, even in districts in which there is little or no competition. While most strong potential candidates cannot match the incumbent in strategic resources, they are as strong as incumbents in their personal qualities. Our informant data indicate clearly that potential candidates' quality—both strategic and personal—is related to their chances of winning. The fact that higher-quality potential candidates, if only they would run, could make House races more competitive, sustains a widely held view, but it is very important to establish. It demonstrates clearly that the decision of most of these high-quality potential candidates not to run is an important reason why House races are not more competitive.

Many high-quality potential candidates might respond to the claim that their entry into their local House race would make it more competitive by saying something like, "Although I might make the race more competitive,

I can't seriously consider running unless I have a reasonable chance of winning." In other words, making a race more competitive is not the same thing as making it competitive. Potential candidates realize that many of the most important factors that affect how competitive a House race will be are out of their hands: Will the popular incumbent decide to run for reelection? Is the partisan makeup of the district favorable or unfavorable? Are national political tides favorable or unfavorable?

What is to be done if we are genuinely interested in making House races more competitive? We suggest a two-pronged approach to the problem. First, serious thought must be given to ways of producing more competition by working on the basic structural factors of incumbency and district partisanship. For example, if ensuring competitive House races is truly in the national interest, public policies that increase our investment in the ability of challengers to come closer to matching the resources that incumbents enjoy is one way of leveling the playing field. Campaign finance reform is a way that public policy might be altered to enhance the strategic resources of challengers. Similarly, anything that encourages the political parties to invest in their House candidates could increase the strategic resources of House challengers as well as move in the direction of producing greater partisan balance in many districts. If significant steps could be taken to reduce the institutional advantages incumbents have over challengers and to produce more districts that are balanced in their partisan makeup, more high-quality candidates would emerge because they would perceive the opportunity in their districts to be more favorable.[30]

The second approach is to think about ways that individual potential candidates might be induced to run, apart from affecting incumbency and district partisanship. We have seen that potential candidates are dissuaded from running because of the personal costs that are entailed in running for and holding high public office. Many of these costs are inherent and cannot be altered. A California potential candidate contemplating a run for the House must anticipate not only the expense and stresses of the campaign in her district. If she wins, she knows that she will place enormous stress on her family and spend endless hours commuting back and forth across the country. That, of course, may be a very high price to pay for the privilege of holding office.

One of the results from our study is that being asked to run seems to matter. Potential candidates who were contacted by their political party or by others[31] and asked to consider entering a House race indicated that they were far more likely to run than were those who had not been actively recruited in these ways (Figure 2-2). These data suggest that various civic, partisan, and community organizations can make a big difference by encouraging strong potential candidates to run. Potential candidates who have received encouragement to run are much more likely to think about running in a given year, and the more encouragement they receive, the better.[32]

Figure 2-2   Contact and Potential Candidates' Chances of Running in 1998

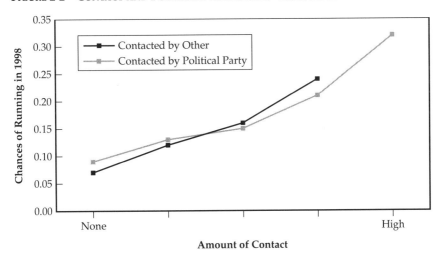

The importance of contact suggests a broader focus on our civic culture as part of the explanation for potential candidates' reticence about running. The value of political institutions to society, and of the people who hold and seek office in them, must be reaffirmed. Americans have always been cynical about politics and politicians, but perhaps our contemporary culture has gone beyond a healthy skepticism. As Martin Frost pointed out, the job of being a congressman or congresswoman is not as attractive as it used to be. Popular culture regularly holds political leaders—and perhaps especially congressional leaders—up to ridicule. If seeking public office is widely regarded as both an unimportant and a dishonorable pursuit, can it be any surprise that individuals with the qualities we seek in our public leaders hesitate? The potential candidates we surveyed are respected, highly skilled, successful people. They have many opportunities outside of politics, and most of our respondents are extremely successful in their private pursuits. Why should they give up the many opportunities they have in their current positions to run for the House? The answer must come in part from a commitment to the public good and a commensurate recognition by the public of the value of high-quality politicians to society.

Appendix: The Candidate Emergence Study

To investigate this decision process, we first had to identify quality potential candidates and to assess their strengths and weaknesses. We began with a survey of politically knowledgeable activists to serve as "informants" in our random sample of congressional districts. We selected political activists in the districts because we believed that they would have a good working knowledge of the politics in their districts and would be able to provide us with information about strong potential candidates in their area, including local business or community leaders who had not yet held elective office. Interestingly, Representative Martin Frost, former chair of the Democratic Congressional Campaign Committee, indicated in a May 7, 1999, interview with us that these are the same types of individuals that the national party contacts to identify individuals the party might recruit to run for a House seat.

Our research design is spelled out in greater detail in Walter J. Stone, L. Sandy Maisel, and Cherie Maestas, "Candidate Emergence in U.S. House Elections," a paper presented at the 1998 Annual Meeting of the American Political Science Association, Boston, September 3–6. We had tested this technique in an exploratory study with encouraging results; the exploratory study is discussed in L. Sandy Maisel and Walter J. Stone, "Determinants of Candidate Emergence in U.S. House Elections: An Exploratory Study," *Legislative Studies Quarterly* 22: 79–96 (1997).

In addition to asking our informants to identify potential candidates in their districts, we asked them to provide systematic information about the characteristics of the candidates they recommended, the political conditions in their districts, and the characteristics of the incumbent representative from the district. Their responses give us a wealth of information about the political context that potential candidates face in the district and a variety of directly comparable measures of potential candidate and incumbent quality.

Our target pool of usable informants for our first survey was 3,573 individuals. Our procedure was to mail a letter explaining the study, followed by a questionnaire, and a reminder postcard. Those who did not respond were mailed a second questionnaire. Because the potential candidate segment of the questionnaire was lengthy and presented respondents with an unusual task, we sent a third mailing to informants who did not respond to either of the first two mailings, asking only for their perceptions of the district and incumbent. Thirty-three percent responded to one of the first two mailings, and another 10 percent responded to the third mailing, for a total of 43 percent.

In the second stage of our research, we surveyed the potential candidates named by the informants. We supplemented this pool with state legislators whose districts overlapped our sample of congressional districts, because the state legislatures represent the largest single source of candidates for the House. We asked these respondents a variety of questions designed to provide information about their perceptions of the district, the incumbent, and factors that might relate to their decision about whether to run for office. Among the questions of interest here, we asked potential candidates to assess their chances of winning their party's nomination and the general election, should they decide to run for the House of Representatives.

We mailed 3,640 surveys to our potential candidates—1,399 to potential candidates named in our informant survey and 2,241 to state legislators whose districts overlapped the sampled congressional districts but who were not named in our informant survey. Our response rate for this survey, again with reminder mailings sent and those responses included, was 33 percent. The response rate was approximately the same for named potential candidates as it was for state legislators who had not been named by our informants.

ACKNOWLEDGMENTS

We are grateful for support from the National Science Foundation for the surveys on which this paper is based (SBR-9515350). We would like to thank our home institutions, Colby College, the University of Colorado, and Texas Tech University for assistance on the project. Stone is currently on leave from the University of Colorado visiting at Stanford University, and thanks the Hoover Institution and the Department of Political Science at Stanford for providing supportive environments in which to work. We would also like to thank the research assistants who have worked on the Candidate Emergence Study, especially Claire Sherman, who discovered a number of the examples used in this chapter.

NOTES

1. State law specifies residency requirements for candidates for office, but none is very restrictive. Contrary to common belief, a member of the House does not need to reside in the district from which he or she is elected, but only in the state.
2. Because we see the skills and resources necessary to be competitive as closely related to those that are required of an effective legislator, high-quality candidates are also likely to be effective representatives. However, note that our definition ignores the interest-basis of political representation. In most democratic theories, the interests of voters are of paramount importance in selecting representatives to serve in the legislature on their behalf. Thus, for example, liberal voters support liberal candidates, while conservative voters back conservative candidates. However, we do not equate "quality" with a particular interest, such as how liberal a prospective candidate is, even though a liberal voter probably would conclude that a "high-quality" candidate must be liberal.
3. See Clyde Wilcox and Wesley Joe, "Dead Law: The Federal Election Finance Regulations, 1974–1996," *PS: Political Science & Politics* 30 (1998): 14–17.
4. Gary C. Jacobson and Samuel Kernell, *Strategy and Choice in Congressional Elections*, 2nd ed. (New Haven: Yale University Press, 1983).
5. Ibid., 31, Table 3-1.

6. Several scholars have refined the Jacobson and Kernell measure by including characteristics of the previous office held, in order to approximate its relationship to winning a House seat (for example, winning a city council election is less an indication of the relevant qualities than winning a state senate seat). See Jon R. Bond, Cary Covington, and Richard Fleisher, "Explaining Challenger Quality in Congressional Elections," *Journal of Politics* 47 (1985): 510–529; Peverill Squire, "Challengers in U.S. Senate Elections," *Legislative Studies Quarterly* 14 (1989): 531–547.

7. Gary F. Moncrief, "Candidate Spending in State Legislative Races," in Joel A. Thompson and Gary F. Moncrief, eds., *Campaign Finance in State Legislative Elections* (Washington, DC: CQ Press, 1998), Table 3-1.

8. Bias is especially a problem in ratings of incumbents because we surveyed equal numbers of Democratic and Republican informants. Thus, for example, Democratic informants in a district held by a Republican incumbent must rate a representative of the opposite party, while Republicans in the same district rate a representative of their own party. There is a tendency, not surprisingly, for informants to rate incumbents in their own party more highly than incumbents in the opposite party. The same tendency exists in informants' ratings of the potential candidates they named, although most informants named potential candidates in their own party. For more information on the problem of partisan bias and the method we use to correct it, see Walter J. Stone and L. Sandy Maisel, "The Not-So-Simple Calculus of Winning: Potential U.S. House Candidates' Nomination and General Election Chances," a paper presented at the 1999 Annual Meeting of the American Political Science Association, Atlanta, September 2–5. This and other papers from the Candidate Emergence Study are available on the study's website at http://socsci.colorado.edu/CES/home.html.

9. Scales run from extremely weak through extremely strong. Entries in the table are percentages of informants who gave at least "somewhat strong" ratings.

10. We did not ask informants to rate incumbents on this item. It is excluded from the Strategic Quality Index, which includes only items asked about both potential candidates and incumbents.

11. This is not to say that *money* is unimportant in House elections. Notice, for instance, that three-quarters of informants rated the potential candidates they named as strong in their ability to raise money. More detailed analysis suggests that the ability to raise money is the single most important factor in explaining potential candidates' chances of winning a House seat. See Walter J. Stone, L. Sandy Maisel, Cherie Maestas, and Sean Evans, "A New Perspective on Candidate Quality in U.S. House Elections," a paper presented at the 1998 Annual Meeting of the Midwest Political Science Association, Chicago, April 14–16.

12. Specifically, we asked the informants to give us their estimate of each potential candidate's chance of winning the party's primary election in 1998, if the candidate were to decide to enter the race. We also asked for their estimated chance of the potential candidate's winning the general election, if that potential candidate were to win the party's nomination. The items are coded on 7-point scales ranging from "Extremely Unlikely" through "Extremely Likely," coded .01 to .99 (as opposed to 0 to 1), to reflect the fact that the end points do not represent a certain expectation of winning or losing. Because winning the House seat requires a candidate to win both the nomination and general election stages, we calculated

an overall estimate for the chances of winning the seat by multiplying together the probability of winning each of the two stages for each potential candidate. See Stone and Maisel, 1999 (note 8). Table 2-2 reports this joint probability.

13. As we would expect, given this argument, strategic and personal qualities are correlated with one another (r = .42).

14. For the purposes of this chapter, we focus on the preconditions for two-party competition in the districts. However, the fact that there is also a sizable number of credible potential candidates in the party of the incumbent is reassuring because it does suggest that a pool of individuals exist who could provide representational choice to voters *within* each party. In reality, intense in-party competition is rare. Only one incumbent, Jay Kim (R-CA), lost the nomination in 1998, and he had been convicted of campaign finance irregularities in his own 1996 election at the time of his 1998 primary defeat.

15. In addition to districts in which no major-party candidate emerged to challenge the incumbent, the other two classifications of districts were defined as "not competitive" (where one major-party candidate got less than 40 percent of the vote) and "competitive" (where both major-party candidates received at least 40 percent).

16. For an interesting study of incumbent quality, see Carl McCurley and Jeffery J. Mondak, "Inspected by #1184063113: The Influence of Incumbents' Competence and Integrity in U.S. House Elections," *American Journal of Political Science* 39 (November 1995): 864–885; Jeffrey J. Mondak, "Competence, Integrity, and the Electoral Success of Congressional Incumbents," *Journal of Politics* 57 (December 1995): 1043–1069.

17. Refer to note 12 for an explanation of how the expected chances of winning were calculated. We asked the same set of questions of potential candidates regarding chances of winning at the two separate stages of the electoral process as we did of the informants.

18. Although potential candidates in the out party did not see it as quite certain. In districts where there turned out to be *no* challenger from their party in 1998, potential candidates saw their chances of winning the nomination as .67—high, but not perfect. By way of contrast, however, *in*-party potential candidates in these same districts saw their chances of winning their party's nomination if they were to run as only .18.

19. It is interesting to speculate about why general election chances against an incumbent are seen by potential candidates as higher than nomination chances. One possible reason is that primary electorates are more predictably loyal to their incumbent than general election voters—that they are less volatile and more difficult to move.

20. For a detailed discussion of the relationships among district partisanship, incumbency, and potential candidates' chances of winning, see Stone and Maisel, 1999 (note 8).

21. L. Sandy Maisel and Walter J. Stone, "Determinants of Candidate Emergence in U.S. House Elections: An Exploratory Study," *Legislative Studies Quarterly* 22 (1997): 79–96.

22. For an account of candidates and candidate plans in Nebraska district 3, see David Kotok and Chris Burbach, "Political Focus Shifts to Senate Hopefuls. With Tom Osborne in the 3rd District House Race, Who Will Seek Bob Kerry's Seat?"

ɔmaha World Herald, January 28, 2000; or Chris Burbach and Jason Gertzen, "3rd District Field Thins after Osborne's Entry," _Omaha World Herald,_ January 28, 2000, Bulldog Edition. The latter article also highlights how the entry of a strong candidate can be a deterrent to other potential candidates. A complete list of candidates who had filed to run in Nebraska's district 3, and their backgrounds, was drawn from information at http://www.Politics1.com.

23. The mean perceived chances of winning the seat among all potential candidates in our sample is only .19.
24. Frost interview, May 7, 1999.
25. Toner's interviews were conducted with potential candidates considering races for a seat not included in our sample of congressional districts. See Robin Toner, "Willing Contenders at a Premium in Fierce Fight to Rule Congress," _New York Times,_ January 3, 2000, A1, A14.
26. Ibid.
27. Frost interview, May 7, 1999. Presumably what is true for husbands who might run is true with at least equal force for wives who are potential candidates concerned about the impact their decision would have on their husbands' lives and careers.
28. Preliminary analysis of our data suggests that female potential candidates may be especially sensitive to the effect a decision to run would have on their families.
29. L. Sandy Maisel, "The 2000 Election in the U.S.: Can the Voice of the People Be Heard?" Olin Lecture, University of Toronto, February 7, 2000.
30. In arguing for more investment in House challengers, we are not saying that the quality of incumbents is low. Indeed, we believe quite the opposite. For one thing, we are persuaded by our own informants that the overall quality of incumbents is remarkably high. For another, others have argued persuasively that the process of election and reelection enhances the quality of incumbent representatives in Congress. See Mondak, "Competence, Integrity, and Electoral Success"; John Zaller, "Politicians as Prize Fighters: Electoral Selection and Incumbency Advantage," in J. G. Geer, ed., _Politicians and Party Politics_ (Baltimore: Johns Hopkins University Press, 1998). Our concern is not with low-quality incumbents; it is with the absence of competition in House elections.
31. We asked potential candidates to indicate whether they had been contacted about running by various party organizations (local, state, or national). The party contact series in Figure 2-2 is composed of these questions, ranging from those not contacted at all through those contacted by all four of the party organizational entities we asked about. The "contacted by other" series is composed of questions asking about recruitment by community leaders, interest groups, and family members.
32. Care must be taken with the results in Figure 2-2, since contact is likely to be sensitive to the opportunity in the district and to other factors that relate to the potential candidate's chances of winning. Nonetheless, our preliminary analysis of the importance of contact suggests that its effects hold up well with controls for other factors that also motivate individuals to run.

3

Competing for Cash: The Individual Financiers of Congressional Elections

BENJAMIN A. WEBSTER / CLYDE WILCOX

PAUL S. HERRNSON / PETER L. FRANCIA

JOHN C. GREEN / LYNDA POWELL

On any given weekend, scores of House candidates are out raising money. In California, one incumbent may be hosting a dinner that costs $500 per plate. Many of those in attendance will be executives of companies that have business before that incumbent's committee. In Wisconsin, a candidate may be addressing a local meeting of the Sierra Club, hoping that its members will contribute to her campaign and also volunteer their services. In Washington, DC, a powerful committee chair may attend a political action committee (PAC) fund-raising cocktail party for a freshman member of his committee, thereby greatly increasing the total raised. In New York, a candidate who plans to launch a challenge to an incumbent may be looking over her finances, trying to determine just how much of her own money she can spend to launch the campaign. In Texas, Christian conservative leaders may be trying to persuade a local business leader active in an evangelical church to run for office, promising him money and volunteers to aid the campaign.

Individual donors, especially those who make large contributions, play important roles in congressional elections. Their support, or lack thereof, influences whether some potential candidates run for the House. Their participation in elections as grass-roots volunteers and fund-raisers can increase a campaign's competitiveness. Most importantly, their contributions are a critical factor in determining the viability of most congressional candidates. This chapter examines the demographic characteristics, political attitudes, motives, and decision-making criteria of individual large donors, and the impact that these factors have on the probability they will be solicited to contribute to a congressional candidate and on the amounts they actually contributed to House candidates in the 1996 elections. In addition, we discuss the individuals' opinions of the campaign finance system they help fuel and some major proposals for reforming it.

MONEY AND POLITICS

Running a credible campaign for the U.S. House of Representatives requires a substantial amount of money. Nonincumbents must generally raise $800,000 or more to compete; incumbents may need much less money if their opponent is weak, but are able to raise much more for a truly competitive election. The race for votes is therefore preceded and paralleled by a race for cash, which frequently occupies a great deal of the candidates' time. Although candidates with the most money do not always win, candidates who cannot raise large sums almost always lose. Moreover, as contribution limits have remained fixed by law, the cost of campaigning has increased steadily, and as a result the race for resources has grown more demanding.

This competition for money is a uniquely American process. In most other industrialized democracies, political parties receive monies from the government or private sources, and distribute those resources to the candidates who "stand for" the party. Candidates need not worry about soliciting contributions, although they are almost entirely reliant on the beneficence of the party for their campaign resources. In the United States, candidates assemble their own financial constituencies in both primary and general elections. If the primary election is contested, party committees are in most cases neutral, although they may offer advice to strong candidates. In the general election, candidates can count on their parties for at least some (and occasionally substantial) support, but they must also continue to work to raise money for their campaigns.

Political activists all have their favorite slogans that emphasize the importance of money: Money is the mother's milk of politics; Money makes the campaign run on time; Money is a candidate's best friend. The ubiquity of slogans about campaign cash points to the widespread belief among politicians, journalists, and academics that money is vitally important in congressional elections.

Money is important mainly for what it buys. Money buys public opinion research, which can identify an opponent's weakness or the candidate's greatest strength. Focus groups and polling done early in a campaign help candidates set their strategy. Polling identifies the issues most critical to voters, and enables campaigns to track trends in public support and to respond quickly. Without polling, candidates must rely on their own instincts, which are occasionally right but more often wrong.

Money also buys advice on strategy and tactics. Campaigns with sufficient resources can hire full-time campaign managers, and can retain the services of consulting firms that supply general campaign advice, assist with free media, and help design advertisements for television, radio, and direct mail. Many media firms work closely with polling consultants to track the impact of advertisements.

In addition, money buys volume in political communications. In many congressional districts, this means television spots that can air repeatedly in the weeks before an election. In districts where television is inefficient or too costly, money buys targeted radio spots, direct-mail appeals, and campaign literature for distribution in select precincts by volunteers.

Some candidates have access to other resources that can help ameliorate the effects of inadequate funding. There may be a key issue that has the attention of the free media, or a cadre of enthusiastic volunteers, or free or cheap communication channels through interest-group newsletters or church networks. These resources can sometimes help an under-funded candidate carry the day, especially in an election with national trends or in a district with favorable partisanship. Yet few candidates who face real competition win without raising significant sums: In 1998 the smallest amount spent by a winning challenger—Mark Green (R-WI)—was almost $850,000.

THE RULES OF THE GAME

The money chase is regulated by a Byzantine set of rules and regulations that have evolved out of the original Federal Election Campaign Act of 1974 (FECA). There are limits on the amounts that institutions and individual contributors can give to candidates, although there are ways for potential contributors to circumvent these limits. These regulations direct money into particular channels, and also affect the way that candidates raise money.[1]

Interest groups can form political action committees (PACs) and give up to $10,000 to a candidate who runs in both a primary and a general election campaign. PACs can also spend unlimited amounts to independently advocate the election or defeat of a candidate, and interest groups can spend from their treasuries unlimited amounts to advocate issues that are associated with particular candidates in ads that can feature the picture of candidates but do not *explicitly* call for their election or defeat. In addition, interest groups can give unlimited amounts of "soft money," which is reused and spent outside of the FECA's regulatory requirements, to party committees to help build the party or finance state and local campaigns; in practice some of this money gets earmarked for House candidates.[2]

Party committees can give money directly to candidates, and can spend money in coordination with the candidate's campaigns. The amount of party contributions and coordinated expenditures are limited by law, but parties can also spend unlimited amounts to advocate issues or even to advocate the election or defeat of candidates if that spending is not coordinated with the candidate's campaign.

Individuals can give up to $2,000 to candidates who run in both the general election and in primaries. Individual contributions in House races are generally raised through networks of solicitors, who invite donors to events such as dinners or cookouts. Candidates also make personal appeals to potential donors for individual contributions. Some individual contributions are coordinated by interest groups, which "bundle" individual donations and give them to the candidate. A few highly visible, ideological House candidates can raise money through impersonal mail or phone solicitations that stress that candidate's positions on certain issues.

Finally, candidates can contribute money to their own campaigns, or loan money that might be repaid at a later date. There are no limits on the amounts that candidates can invest in their own campaigns, giving wealthy Americans a substantial advantage in seeking election to the House and especially to the Senate. Although few incumbents need to give to their own campaigns, many challengers and open-seat candidates use their own money to launch their campaigns.[3]

The campaign for resources is a decidedly uneven one, with incumbents enjoying enormous advantages over challengers.[4] In 1998, incumbents in jeopardy raised more than a million dollars on average, whereas their challengers raised slightly more than $600,000. Yet only 94 House incumbents faced any real competition, and the more than 212 incumbents who were easy winners enjoyed an even greater fund-raising advantage over their opponents. Indeed, the entire process of raising money differs greatly for incumbents and challengers, as do the sources of funds. Open-seat candidates—candidates running for a seat vacated by a retiring incumbent—differ from both incumbents and challengers in their fund-raising.

FUND-RAISING BY INCUMBENTS, CHALLENGERS, AND OPEN-SEAT CANDIDATES

Incumbents are generally experienced politicians who know their district well, and who work hard to remain popular with constituents. Incumbents who seek reelection begin with substantial advantages. They have many advantages by virtue of their office, and can use those resources to build support among the electorate. Incumbents can often feed sympathetic stories to local newspapers, and in their frequent visits to the district they can cultivate their personal "home style," which helps them build a loyal constituency.[5] They have legislative correspondents to answer district mail, press secretaries to publicize their efforts in the media, and other official perks that are worth roughly $1 million per year.[6] All of this provides incumbents with significant name recognition, an important voting cue. Many incumbents retain a sizable "war chest" in the bank to deter potential challengers, and spend money from that account to mail campaign communications to the district and to cement support among constituents.[7]

In addition, incumbents can often raise significant amounts from individuals. Nearly all incumbents organize fund-raising committees through which lobbyists and other supporters agree to help solicit funds for the candidate.

Incumbents with strong ideological appeals can raise individual contributions through direct-mail solicitations, although this is far more common for senators than for members of the House.

In 1998, incumbents in competitive House races in both parties raised an average of more than $1,000,000 apiece.[8] Incumbents who were certain of victory raised an average of more than $500,000. PACs are a major source of funds for incumbents, providing a third of the money for GOP incumbents and nearly half of the money for safe Democratic incumbents in 1998. But individual contributions were the largest single source of money for incumbents of both parties, constituting more than half of all funds. Nearly a third of House incumbent receipts came from individual contributions in amounts of $200 or more.

Most incumbents are in little danger of defeat in any given election, for they do not usually face an experienced or well-known challenger. When a real challenge does arise, incumbents have the ability to raise significant sums from institutional actors. Most incumbents hold PAC fund-raising events, where PAC officials deliver a contribution to the campaign of the incumbent and then mingle or eat and drink. Powerful incumbents can sometimes hold events to which the required contribution is $5,000, or in some cases $10,000 (the maximum contribution for any candidate running in a primary and general election). These fund-raising events may be timed to coincide with consideration of particular legislation of interest to the PAC community. Many PAC representatives report that when they get such an invitation they do not believe they can say no.[9] Incumbents can also usually rely on party committees to provide significant resources if the race promises to be close.[10]

Democratic representative David Price's fund-raising efforts are typical of those of an incumbent who is routinely involved in a tough reelection campaign. Campaigns in Price's North Carolina congressional district tend to be expensive and hard fought. Price first won the seat in 1986, lost it during the Republican tidal wave of 1994, and then reclaimed it in 1996. In 1998 Price faced Republican challenger Thomas Roberg, a wealthy North Carolina businessman and former chairman of the Wake County Republican Party. Price considered Roberg one of the most formidable opponents he had ever faced, and he was also concerned that a redistricting challenge underway in a neighboring district could alter the composition of his seat in a way that would favor the Republican. Price prepared for what he anticipated and what proved to be a competitive campaign by amassing a large campaign war chest—nearly $1.3 million. He collected almost 20 percent of those funds before Roberg raised any money at all. Price collected about one-third of his funds from PACs; most of the remainder came from individuals. Individual contributions of $200 or more comprised an important portion of Price's resources, accounting for about one-third of his total receipts. Price's aggressive fund-raising enabled him to set a personal record in 1998 and helped him defeat Roberg by a 10 percent vote margin.[11]

For challengers, fund-raising is a more difficult enterprise. Some challengers lack any experience in elective office or other characteristics that would make them strong candidates; these challengers have difficulty in raising money from any source except their own checkbooks. More promising candidates—state legislative incumbents, prominent business or civic leaders, and others with name recognition in the district—can raise money from institutions and individuals if they can persuade them that they have a chance of winning. Thus in order to *raise* money, challengers must *have* money: to rent the services of consultants, to conduct polls showing the incumbent's vulnerabilities, to do some preliminary advertising to increase their name recognition in order to convince PACs, party officials, and major donors to invest in their campaign.

This initial money, often referred to as "seed" money, comes from a variety of sources.[12] Candidates usually ask their friends, family, and neighbors to give early to the campaign. Some PACs, especially those sponsored by labor unions and women's groups, give early money to help launch campaigns. EMILY's List, a PAC that supports pro-choice Democratic women candidates, is one of the best known of these PACs. Yet many candidates finance the early stages of their campaigns from their own resources—loaning or contributing substantial amounts of money to their own campaigns.[13]

Once a challenger has launched a credible campaign, he or she can appeal to the same sources as incumbents—to PACs, party committees, and individuals. Yet because challengers seldom win, access-oriented PACs and individuals are reluctant to contribute to even those who run solid campaigns. As a result, competitive challengers usually raise much less than the vulnerable incumbents they are hoping to defeat.

In marked contrast to the sources of receipts for incumbents, challengers raise much less of their money from PACs. The typical challenger, who has little prospect of winning, raises less than 14 percent of his or her funds from PACs; challengers who are in close races do only somewhat better at around 19 percent. Like incumbents, challengers raise approximately one-third of their money in individual contributions of more than $200, and additional funds from smaller donations. The amounts of money challengers invest in their own campaigns varies greatly, but many challengers in close races loan or donate in excess of $100,000.

Thomas Roberg's 1998 fund-raising effort is illustrative of that of a challenger in a close contest. Roberg raised approximately $472,000, plus an additional $63,000 worth of coordinated campaign services from the Republican Party. Individual donors provided him with roughly half of his total campaign dollars, and most of their donations were made in amounts of $200 or more. PACs provided Roberg with less than 8 percent of his receipts, and the candidate loaned the campaign $180,000, about 38 percent of its total funds. To help launch his campaign, Roberg provided $50,000 of his own funds.[14]

Open seats are created when incumbents retire. Some open seats occur in districts where one party has an overwhelming advantage, but in general open seats are more competitive than incumbent–challenger races. Many of the strongest potential candidates choose to bide their time until an incumbent retires, because they know that if they challenge the incumbent they will almost certainly lose. Although open-seat candidates often need to scramble to line up seed money, it is far easier for them to raise funds than for challengers. The typical open-seat contestant in a close contest in 1998 raised almost $880,000 and was able to pry open the coffers of institutional sources of funds. Whereas the typical challenger in a competitive 1998 election contest raised approximately $121,000 in PAC contributions, open-seat candidates with good prospects raised an average of almost $282,000 (almost 30 percent) from PACs. Open-seat candidates also raised large sums from individuals who make large donations, many of whom had ties to or shared economic incentives with these institutions. They collected an average of $345,000 in individual contributions of $200 or more, and another $146,000 in individual contributions of less than $200.

The fund-raising efforts of Democrat Dave Wu and Republican Molly Bordonaro in the 1998 race in Oregon's 1st congressional district are typical of candidates locked in a hotly contested open-seat campaign. Each candidate raised approximately $1.5 million, with Wu collecting $110,000 more than Bordonaro. PACs provided Wu with $361,000 in contributions and gave his Republican opponent $396,000. Individuals contributed about $1 million to each of the candidates. Bordonaro raised almost three-fourths of her individual donations in contributions of $200 or more, whereas Wu collected about two-thirds of his individual donations in such large amounts. The two political parties invested about $73,000 each in the contest—approximately the legal maximum in contributions and coordinated expenditures. Wu ultimately prevailed in this high-spending contest, squeezing out a 3-point victory over Bordonaro.

Clearly, fund-raising is easier for incumbents and open-seat contestants, who are generally thought to have a significant chance of winning, and much more difficult for challengers, who are likely to lose. Fund-raising shortfalls make it difficult for candidates to introduce themselves to voters and to wage competitive campaigns, thereby completing the loop.

INDIVIDUAL CONTRIBUTORS IN HOUSE RACES

The campaign for resources has received a great deal of attention from the media, from reformers, and from academics. The role of institutional actors in financing House elections has been the major focus of reformers. In the 1980s, many reformers charged that political action committees corrupted Congress with their voluminous campaign contributions. By the late 1990s, PACs were recast as model citizens that disclosed their receipts and expenditures and abided by the original FECA limits. In contrast, soft money from interest-group treasuries, and issue ads by parties and groups, were seen as potential sources of corruption.

Many reform proposals are directed toward increasing the role of individual contributions in funding House elections, either by limiting institutional money or by providing incentives for candidates to seek contributions from constituents, or for individuals to give to candidates. Such reforms assume that money coming from individual contributors is somehow more "pure" than institutional money—because individual donors are thought to give in response to local issues and electoral concerns, not in exchange for material benefits from legislative action.

However, individual donors are already the single most important source of money for House candidates. Their contributions typically constitute more than 50 percent of the funds raised by major-party candidates running for contested seats. Large individual contributions—those of $200 or more—usually account for roughly 35 percent.

In order to learn more about the characteristics, motives, and contribution behavior of individual donors to House races, we conducted a survey of a random sample of large contributors to House and Senate races who made at least one contribution of $200 or more.[15] Surveys were mailed to more than 2,000 individuals who contributed $200 or more to House or Senate candidates. The response rate was 50 percent, resulting in 1,118 observations. We also interviewed an illustrative sample of 35 large donors to obtain some in-depth information about the factors that influence their contributing decisions and political behavior. Finally, we interviewed a bipartisan group of six finance directors, who earn their living raising money for congressional candidates. In this chapter we consider only those respondents who reported giving to a House candidate in the 1995–1996 campaigns. (See the Appendices to this chapter for more information on the survey).

THE INDIVIDUAL DONOR POOL IN HOUSE RACES

Contributors to House elections constitute a relatively stable pool of donors; some give occasionally to candidates or party organizations, others give in most elections to all types of campaign actors. More than half (55 percent) of 1996 House donors reported that they gave to House candidates in most elections. Fully 70 percent reported giving in most elections to a presidential, House, Senate, state, or local candidate, or to a party committee. More than one-third give in most elections to at least four of these five types of actors. Two-thirds report that they give at least in some elections to all five types. Few House donors give only to House candidates: 1 percent did so in 1996. Based on responses to these survey questions, we have divided House donors into three sets: those who give habitually to all kinds of candidates and parties; those who give regularly to a few types of actors but not to all; and those who give only occasionally to any type of candidate and party committee.

Habitual donors give early and give often. One conservative Republican man who owns a small business told us: "I give through a number of venues. I give through organized committees: the presidential committee, House Republicans, Senate Republicans, the State of Connecticut Republican Party, and several PACs." A liberal Democratic woman who is a community organizer told us: "I am a major campaign contributor. My family was wealthy and I was brought up to feel that I had an obligation to help the less fortunate. I do a lot of volunteer activity and give lots of money to charity. And campaign donations are just another side of this effort." A Democratic lobbyist, one of the biggest donors in the country, told us: "I'm a 'max out' contributor for many years. My wife gives something like $125,000 and I give $150,000 total."

These donors tell us something important about habitual donors. They are wealthy, and give not only to politics but also to charity, community organizations, and other causes. They give in politics to all kinds of candidates, party committees, and PACs, and give substantial contributions. To "max out" to a candidate, PAC, or party committee means to give the maximum legal amount—$25,000 per year to federal candidates, party committees, and PACs. Many habitual donors do just that, and give soft money. Habitual donors enjoy giving, as do their friends and neighbors.

Regular donors are more likely to give a few donations to candidates of both parties in most elections. One conservative business executive who identified with neither party told us: "I give modestly to pursue my interests with the government. I'm not sure I like doing this, but that is the world we live in." A liberal Democrat who retired from the federal bureaucracy noted: "I do contribute modestly to a few candidates, both in my state and outside it. I contributed to a presidential candidate, but the last time I sent a note back saying that if they worked on getting a campaign finance reform passed then I'll continue to contribute. I have supported candidates in both parties."

The common themes from these two regular donors are that they give small amounts to a few candidates, and that they do so with some reluctance. These donors give often enough to appear on the lists of potential donors that candidates solicit, but they are not a reliable source of funds.

Finally, occasional donors give in some elections to a few, or more commonly to one candidate. One older Republican man told us: "I don't contribute much, maybe a little to a candidate I know." A Democratic homemaker said, "I'm not really a campaign contributor. I give a small amount very occasionally when a friend asks. I mostly say no." Both of these donors give small amounts in some elections, usually no more than a few hundred dollars, when a friend or someone they know is running. Such donors are only a peripheral part of the donor pool, and cannot be easily mobilized by candidates who lack personal connections.

In the previous quotes, we sought to present a balance of men and women, Republicans and Democrats. Yet the donor pool is not evenly balanced; instead it is overwhelmingly white, predominantly male, disproportionately older, well educated, and quite affluent (see Table 3-1). More than three in four are men, and nearly all are white. More than 40 percent have incomes of over $250,000; in 1996 fewer than 2 percent of the general public had similar incomes. Donors are also disproportionately affiliated with mainline Protestant denominations, and are heavily conservative and Republican. Candidates of both parties must appeal to this pool to fund their campaigns.

There are important differences between those donors who give in some elections to some types of candidates and those who give in most elections to all types (see Table 3-2 on page 52). Habitual donors are slightly more likely to be white, male, older, mainline Protestants, and conservative Republicans. They are also wealthier but not better educated than regular donors, suggesting that the most frequent donors are from business rather than from professional occupations. Habitual donors are also far more likely than other contributors to be strong partisans, whereas occasional donors are more likely to be independent.

Candidates solicit contributions from habitual and regular donors, and from individuals outside of the donor pool, who have never before given money in a congressional election. They ask friends and neighbors, associates at work or church, and relatives to give to their campaigns, and many of these prospective donors will agree although they have never given before. Once these individuals have given, however, they are likely to be asked again by other candidates. Some will agree and become occasional donors; others will refuse and never give again.

No successful candidate can fund a campaign entirely from donors outside of the regular pool, however. Successful candidates must also appeal to continuing members of the donor pool, especially to regular and habitual donors, who are more likely to give and who give larger average contributions. Habitual donors gave on average nearly $2,500 to House and Senate candidates in 1998, while occasional donors gave less than $700. Candidates therefore move beyond their circle of close supporters, and ask habitual donors to give to their campaigns. Habitual donors are asked to give by many more candidates than are occasional donors. More than half of all habitual donors were asked in 1998 to give to six or more candidates, and nearly one in four gave to that many candidates. In contrast, more than half of occasional donors gave to only one candidate, although most were asked to give by two or more candidates.

When candidates ask contributors to give, they often ask them to solicit additional contributions from their friends and associates. Fully 45 percent of occasional donors have at least once in their lives solicited contributions for at least one congressional candidate, as have three in four habitual donors.

TABLE 3-1   THE BACKGROUNDS AND ATTITUDES OF LARGE DONORS (%)

	ALL	OCCASIONAL	REGULAR	HABITUAL
Male	77	70	79	81
White	96	94	96	97
Education				
Some college or less	17	22	14	15
Graduate/law/med degree	47	42	54	45
Income				
Less than $100k	18	26	17	13
$250k or more	43	32	42	54
Age				
Under 45	14	22	11	13
46–60	42	41	50	35
61+	43	38	39	52
Church Attendance				
More than weekly	9	12	6	10
Weekly	26	28	22	29
Monthly	17	12	18	19
Few times a year	25	24	25	25
Seldom/never	23	23	28	18
Religious Tradition				
Mainline Protestant	42	31	41	51
Evangelical Protestant	11	16	9	9
Catholic	22	27	22	16
Jew	12	14	11	11
Secular	8	6	12	7
Region				
Northeast	23	21	25	22
Midwest	20	22	20	19
West	21	23	21	20
South	36	34	34	39
Partisanship				
Democrat	31	26	32	33
Independent	20	29	20	9
Republican	50	45	47	58
Ideology				
Liberal	30	29	33	28
Moderate	18	21	16	16
Conservative	52	50	51	56
(N)	(946)	(276)	(367)	(303)

Source: The House and Senate Contributor Study.

TABLE 3-2   LARGE DONORS AS CAMPAIGN CONTRIBUTORS AND SOLICITORS (%)

	ALL	OCCASIONAL	REGULAR	HABITUAL
Asked to give in 1996 by				
1 candidate	11	15	13	2
2–5 candidates	55	67	53	46
6–10 candidates	19	11	19	26
11 or more candidates	16	7	15	25
Number of candidates in 1996 reported given to				
1 candidate	33	54	38	7
2–5 candidates	55	44	52	70
6–10 candidates	6	1	6	12
11 or more candidates	6	1	4	12
Asked others to give to				
Presidential candidate	40	22	36	62
Party committee	31	14	26	54
Congressional candidate	64	45	70	74
PAC	31	17	33	42
(N)	(946)	(276)	(367)	(303)

Source: The House and Senate Contributor Study.

Of course, this does not mean that these donors were deeply involved in campaign fund-raising—many doubtless have asked one friend to give to a candidate. This surprising rate of solicitation needs further study, but it does suggest the importance of approaching the habitual and regular donors in the contributor pool, for they are quite willing to ask others to give.

A METHOD TO THOSE MOTIVES

Candidates must approach the pool for contributions, asking citizens to part with money that they could spend in many enjoyable ways. Candidates therefore must tailor their appeals to donors, emphasizing their assets and attempting to engage the motives that led the donors to become involved in politics. The donor pool is comprised of contributors with a mix of motives. Most donors claim to give because of purposive motives—they want to influence the outcome of an election or to influence public policy (see Table 3-3). A far smaller number are willing to admit giving for material benefits—for business reasons, or because it is expected of someone in their position. Fewer still say they give for solidary motives—an enjoyment of the social contacts that occur at fund-raising events, or a sense of recognition. The distribution of

TABLE 3-3 LARGE DONORS' MOTIVES FOR MAKING CAMPAIGN CONTRIBUTIONS (%)

	ALL	OCCASIONAL	REGULAR	HABITUAL
Purposive Motives				
Influence policies	62	56	61	68
Influence election outcome	63	57	62	69
Material Motives				
Expected of me	4	4	4	4
Business reasons	9	8	8	10
Solidary Motives				
Sense of recognition	1	1	1	2
Social contacts	3	2	3	3
Response to Solicitations				
Give often when asked by a				
Friend or Relative	28	25	23	39
Coworker	13	11	14	14
Business associate	11	7	10	15
Church associate	2	1	1	4
Member of social group	4	1	4	7
Member of political group	12	3	9	23
Party activist	12	5	6	26
Candidate	32	13	33	48
Candidate's staff	9	3	7	16
(N)	(946)	(276)	(367)	(303)

Notes: The columns record the percent of individuals who stated that each factor was very or always important to their contribution decisions.

Source: The House and Senate Contributor Study.

these motives does not vary greatly from occasional to habitual donors; instead, habitual donors are simply more motivated overall. Of course, it is important to bear in mind that it is socially acceptable to admit to giving to influence an election, much less so to admit to giving for business motives. Thus the survey data probably underestimate business giving.

Different candidates may attract contributions from contributors with different motives. Committee and subcommittee chairs on important committees, such as Ways and Means and Appropriations, are more likely than other candidates to attract contributions from donors interested in material benefits; more ideological candidates who take uncompromising positions on issues such as abortion are more likely to attract contributions from donors with purposive motives. Contributors to candidates who are ideologically extreme are primarily motivated by purposive benefits, whereas those who gave to candidates with control of the congressional agenda were distinctive in their strong material motives.

Fund-raising is often a matter of finding the right solicitor. Different types of solicitors are more successful with different types of donors. Occasional donors are mobilized by personal solicitations from friends and relatives—the random ties that lead them to play a role in financing some but not many campaigns. Indeed, occasional donors give more frequently in response to solicitations by friends and family than they do to requests by the candidate herself. Habitual donors also respond to requests by friends and family—more often, in fact, than do occasional donors—but they are especially likely to give when asked by the candidate, by a member of a political group, or by a party activist. Habitual donors are simply more likely to say yes to all solicitors, and thus are more often the target of solicitations.

Yet even habitual contributors say no to some solicitations. More than half of all habitual donors report being asked to give by more than six candidates, but fewer than one in four gave to that many candidates. Indeed, habitual donors say no to more solicitations than do occasional donors, because they receive many more requests to give. How do contributors choose which candidates will receive their largess?

Donors make their decisions based on five general criteria: business; specific issues and a desire to influence Congress; party and ideological competition; personal networks; and local networks and candidate friendship. Some consider whether a candidate can help or hurt their business. One such donor told us: "I give modestly to gain access to the political process. My business is heavily regulated, and it is important that we be treated fairly, both my firm and my industry. Most people have no idea how hard it is to get bureaucrats and legislators to pay attention, and being part of the process helps." Another donor, a retired defense contractor, described his giving while he was part of the firm: "I always saw my giving as part of a bigger program: the donations helped create the kind of Congress where our industry would be taken seriously. Then our lobbyists could make their case. Sometimes we lost fair and square; other times liberals would ignore us and mistreat us. The [defense] industry is easy to attack."

Others decide to give based on the candidates' and their opponent's views on specific policy issues. One such contributor described his decision rules as this: "To me the bottom line is environmental policy: If we don't stop despoiling the air and the water, there will be no political system to worry about in the future. So, I have a kind of test for candidates, namely, where do they stand on the environment? Now this is a fairly complicated thing because there are lots of environmental issues. My evaluation is sort of a sum of issues I care about."

Still others think about ideology and party more generally, and try to direct their contributions to those close elections that can increase their party's representation in Congress. One ideological donor explained, "I make campaign contributions for one reason and one reason only: to influence the philosophy of government. I look for candidates who share my perspective.

If a politician won't come clean on their basic philosophy, then no money from me."

Some donors decide whether to say yes to a solicitation not primarily because of the candidate, but rather because of who asked them. Some are embedded in personal networks, and give because the solicitor is a friend, or perhaps is someone they cannot say no to. Others are involved in specifically local networks, where they give to the local candidate they know personally. One locally oriented contributor noted: "I give politically when I feel the [local candidate] deserves the position and I feel they will do a good job. I want the best person representing me in Congress, someone who takes care of the folks back home. We all pay taxes and we should get our share back from Washington. The federal government can be a real pain, and every area needs a good ambassador to the federal government. So I want the best person we can get."

In general, most contributors report that they consider candidates' ideology, their position on specific issues, the unsavory nature of their opponents, and whether they know the candidate personally or if the candidate is from their district (see Table 3-4 on page 56). Occasional donors are comparatively more likely to consider the candidate's stand on specific issues, and whether the candidate is from the district. Habitual donors are especially likely to consider party—more than 250 percent as likely as are occasional donors. They are also distinctive in considering whether the candidate is in a close race and whether he or she was endorsed by a group the contributor supports. Habitual donors are also somewhat more likely than other donors to consider whether the candidate is likely to win and is friendly to the contributor's industry. In general, however, habitual donors are more likely to mention every factor as being important, perhaps reflecting their greater involvement in contributing and the fact that they are more frequently solicited.

Most habitual donors are highly partisan donors who give for purposive motives, who respond to solicitations by party and group activists, and who consider the candidate's party, ideology, the closeness of the race, and group endorsements. In addition, there is a smaller set of habitual donors who are business-minded contributors motivated by material benefits, who respond to appeals by business associates or the candidate themselves, and who consider whether the candidate is friendly to an industry and can win.

PREDICTING CONTRIBUTION ACTIVITY

Contributors to House elections differ in how many candidates ask them to give, and in the total amounts they give in response to those solicitations. Demographic characteristics, ideology, donor motives, religion, and decision-making criteria all may influence how often contributors are asked to give

TABLE 3-4   LARGE DONORS' DECISION-MAKING CRITERIA (%)

	ALL	OCCASIONAL	REGULAR	HABITUAL
Business Criteria				
So business treated fairly	23	19	26	22
People in my line of work are giving	4	4	4	5
Candidate friendly to industry	25	18	26	29
Specific Issues/Influence Congress				
Candidate position on specific issue	35	32	38	35
Opponent is bad	49	45	51	51
Group has endorsed	13	8	13	16
Candidate's seniority, committee, or leadership	7	6	7	8
Party and Ideological Competition				
Candidate ideology	70	67	70	74
Candidate's party	32	19	30	46
Candidate is in close race	26	22	21	36
Personal Networks				
Asked by someone known	26	27	21	30
Candidate is likely to win	7	5	7	10
Asked by someone couldn't say no to	10	10	9	11
Local Networks/Candidate Friendship				
Candidate from district	66	65	67	65
Know candidate personally	49	47	46	55
Involves an event	4	3	4	5
(N)	(946)	(276)	(367)	(303)

Notes: The figures report the percentage of large donors who indicate that the criteria are almost always important in making their contribution decisions. There is some overlap between personal and local networks, such as where donors are asked to contribute by someone they know.

Source: The House and Senate Contributor Study.

and the total amount of their contributions. In addition, those who are asked more often will probably give more money. We use ordinary least squares regression analysis to analyze the impact that these factors have on the number of solicitations that each donor received and the total amounts that they gave in the 1996 House elections.[16]

Clearly, candidates target wealthier potential donors and those who are highly motivated to contribute. These individuals have the wherewithal to give and reasons for doing so. Members of the congressional donor pool who have annual incomes of less than $50,000 were, on average, asked to give by slightly more than four candidates in the 1996 elections, while the wealthiest donors, who had incomes of over $500,000, were asked to contribute by approximately eight candidates.

Women are asked to give by one more candidate on average than are men with similar incomes and attitudes. The rise of PACs that bundle money on behalf of female candidates, including EMILY's List and WISH List, its Republican counterpart, has had a major impact on the number of women who are asked to contribute to congressional campaigns.[17] There are fewer women in the donor pool, but they have emerged as a distinctive donor group that is targeted by certain candidates.

Strong liberals and conservatives, and those who are members of many political groups, often care deeply about the outcome of elections, and may strongly support candidates of a particular party or ideology. Frequently their names appear on the membership lists of many organizations and on the subscription lists of many liberal or conservative publications. Not surprisingly, donors who describe themselves as extremely liberal or extremely conservative, and those who have memberships in many political groups, are solicited significantly more often than are moderate and less politically active donors.

Religion also has an impact on who is solicited for campaign contributions. Jews and secular voters are solicited significantly more often than are Catholics, evangelical Protestants, or mainline Protestants. The Jewish community has traditionally been highly active in American politics, whereas most other religions have only recently begun to organize their flocks.[18] As a result, Jewish donors tend to be on more contributor lists and are asked to donate to political campaigns more than are members of other religions.

Candidates try to solicit contributions from donors who are highly motivated to give, and who might use decision criteria that would lead them to give to that candidate. Donors who are motivated by purposive goals, such as public policy on highly charged issues like abortion or gay rights, are solicited significantly more often than are others. Similarly, donors who belong to personal solicitation networks are asked more often than are other donors, and often in turn ask others to give. This is also true to a lesser extent for donors who contribute because they seek to advance narrow issues or influence the legislative process. The names of both of these sets of donors undoubtedly appear on the Rolodexes of personal solicitors and of numerous direct-mail solicitation lists because of their direct participation in politics and their efforts to influence congressional decision making.

Individuals who give because of local criteria, such as supporting local candidates, by contrast, are solicited significantly less often than are other donors. The parochial focus of their donations explains why their names are not on many politicians' fund-raising lists and why they are solicited for contributions relatively infrequently. In any given election, there is only one candidate from their party in the local House election.

Many of the same factors that influence how frequently large donors are solicited also influence how much they give. First and foremost, however, the number of times that donors are asked to contribute has a major impact on how much money they give (see the second column in Table 3-5). Donors who were asked to contribute by 10 or more candidates in 1996 contributed, on average, $2,620 more overall to House candidates than did those who were only asked to contribute once.

Not surprisingly, wealthier donors contribute more than do their somewhat less affluent counterparts. Those with incomes above $500,000 gave on average nearly $3,500 more than those with incomes of less than $50,000. However, those with higher levels of education actually give less money than other donors with similar incomes. All large donors are well educated, but those who stopped at a bachelor's or master's degree, and were therefore more likely to enter into a business career, contributed more than those with law, medical, or Ph.D. degrees.

Women give less money than men who have been solicited by the same number of candidates. Women are less likely to give in response to any one request, but because they are asked to contribute more often, they typically end up giving almost as much as men.[19]

Similarly, Jewish and secular voters do not contribute more money to congressional candidates than do other large donors who receive the same numbers of solicitations. However, once the fact that Jewish and secular voters receive more solicitations is taken into account, it becomes apparent that these individuals contribute hundreds of dollars more than do members of most other religious groups. Evangelical Protestants, by contrast, are solicited less frequently, but contribute more than do others who are solicited with similar frequency.[20]

Donors with strong motives are distinctive in their giving. Compared with other large donors who receive the same number of solicitations, those who possess strong purposive motives contribute more to House candidates. Those who possess strong solidary motives, on the other hand, contribute significantly fewer dollars. These donors probably contribute less because their giving is motivated by a desire to rub shoulders with candidates and other big donors, yet this social benefit is unlikely to lead them to travel long distances for a fund-raising dinner. Finally, donors who belong to personal solicitation networks and seek to influence the legislative process contributed more money to House candidates than did others—especially individuals who relied heavily on business criteria when selecting candidates for contributions. This suggests that the public image of business donors may be somewhat inaccurate: Not all of them are heads of Fortune 500 companies who spend tens of thousands of dollars to try to influence powerful members of Congress. Rather, many donors who are motivated by business concerns are small-business owners and mid- and low-level executives who contribute relatively modest amounts to congressional candidates.

TABLE 3-5 SOLICITATIONS AND CONTRIBUTIONS IN HOUSE ELECTIONS

	NUMBER OF SOLICITATIONS	TOTAL CONTRIBUTIONS
Income	1.087***	688.934***
	(.167)	(102.014)
Education	−.004	−181.178**
	(.140)	(82.713)
Female	.836***	−478.334
	(.404)	(240.436)
Strength of partisanship	.097	73.85
	(.165)	(97.932)
Strength of ideology	.451***	−11.18
	(.196)	(116.797)
Group attachment	.243***	−6.25
	(.071)	(42.439)
Frequency of church attendance	−.095	145.271
	(.142)	(83.981)
Evangelical protestant	−.317	640.566**
	(.575)	(340.678)
Catholic	−.076	−82.838
	(.447)	(265.003)
Jewish	1.129**	387.676
	(.545)	(324.202)
Secular	1.33**	480.872
	(.682)	(405.646)
Material motive	.115	6.994
	(.188)	(111.645)
Purposive motive	.725***	144.44*
	(.168)	(100.847)
Solidary motive	−.153	−186.071**
	(.173)	(102.392)
Business criteria	−.243	−452.825***
	(.196)	(116.018)
Personal networks	.516***	319.335***
	(.183)	(109.046)
Party/ideology criteria	−.086	−39.496
	(.182)	(108.109)
Local criteria	−.397***	−96.017
	(.168)	(100.224)
Issue/influence Congress criteria	.234*	175.924**
	(.167)	(98.918)
Solicitation		262.02***
		(22.753)
Constant	−1.51	−1703.604***
	(1.198)	(710.680)
(N)	(703)	(699)
R^2	.18	.34

Notes: ***$p \leq .01$; **$p \leq .05$; *$p \leq .10$, one-tailed tests.
Source: The House and Senate Contributor Study.

CAMPAIGN FINANCE REFORM

Americans who make large contributions to House campaigns are far more familiar with the campaign finance system than is the average American, and they hold some strong views about it. Substantial majorities of contributors favor some kind of reform, and nearly one-third believe that the system is broken and must be replaced (see Table 3-6). One occasional donor, a moderate southern Democrat, strongly stated the case for reform: "Campaign finance today has polluted the political system of our country. The whole system is increasingly sick and perverse. We need some radical reform; look at the whole system. The system can't be fixed by tinkering." Yet another habitual donor was more sanguine about the current system: "The [current] regulations are good if people would follow them. We should kick them out of office if they cheat—get money illegally or do anything illegal."

Although an overwhelming majority of contributors think that contributions are a legitimate form of political participation, majorities also believe that candidates pressure donors for money and donors pressure candidates for favors. A liberal Democratic donor defending contributing as legitimate, although she favors reform, states: "Most donors don't give for access, they give for principles. It is the venal few that give donations a bad name."

Yet donors clearly believe that soliciting and fund-raising are excessive.

TABLE 3-6   LARGE DONORS' EVALUATIONS OF CAMPAIGN FINANCE SYSTEM (%)

	ALL	OCCASIONAL	REGULAR	HABITUAL
Current System is				
Broken	31	31	34	26
Has problems	45	52	44	41
Sound/some change	22	14	21	31
Sound/no change	2	3	1	2
Agree or strongly agree that				
Contributions are a legitimate part of the system	87	75	91	92
Candidates pressure donors for money	80	84	81	75
Donors pressure candidates for favors	58	65	60	51
Most donors seek access	54	56	54	50
Most donors motivated by ideology	55	48	53	65
Money is biggest factor in elections	55	60	56	48
(N)	(946)	(276)	(367)	(303)

Source: The House and Senate Contributor Study.

A retired defense contractor and very conservative Republican told us: "Because I am so active in politics and give a lot of money to many candidates, I am constantly solicited. It really has gotten out of hand. These days politicians are scared and they think they need more money to hedge against risk. They are wrong, of course. What they need instead is a clear program: That is what raises the money and wins elections." Another very large donor told us: "During a campaign, I am badgered constantly and it really angers me. That is why so many big donors want some kind of reform—to keep the fundraising below the level of harassment." Contributors also thought that the insistent fund-raising distracts legislators from their real business. One retired government employee told us: "There should be some way of limiting contributions or limiting the need for contributions because people are constantly soliciting money for campaigns. Senator [X] is still soliciting money to pay off his campaign and it is taking away from what he was elected to do. The whole fund-raising thing has gotten way out of hand."

Habitual donors are more positive toward the current system than are occasional donors. One-third of all habitual donors think that the current system needs at most minor reform, whereas only 17 percent of occasional donors are this sanguine. Habitual donors are more likely to believe that contributors are motivated by ideology than by access, whereas this ordering is reversed among occasional donors. Nevertheless, the strongest conclusion is that a majority of all types of donors are critical of the campaign finance system.

There is strong support for spending caps, limits on TV ads, and a ban on soft money. A sizable majority of occasional donors favored a ban on PAC contributions as well, although only a plurality of regular and habitual donors supported this reform (see Table 3-7 on page 62). In each case, habitual donors are less likely to favor limits than are occasional donors.

One northeastern liberal Democratic woman expressed strong support for limiting spending. "It is obscene the amount of money that is spent on campaigns. One spends because the other spends. I would like to see the amount of money diminish in getting politicians back in office." A retired insurance salesman and very conservative Republican agreed: "Cutting spending would make a difference because then candidates would not need to raise so much money.... I really wish the volume of fund-raising and costs of the system could be reduced."

Only a minority of respondents favored public subsidies in the way of funds or free television, and this does not vary much across categories of giving. Even smaller minorities supported reforms that would increase the limits for individual or party contributions, or eliminate limits altogether and require stricter disclosure. Such reforms were slightly more popular among habitual donors than among occasional givers.

One lawyer-lobbyist who raises a lot of campaign money voiced practical objections to some types of public subsidies: "My problem with free time is that it doesn't work a lot of times. For example, in New York, you are

TABLE 3-7   LARGE DONORS' SUPPORT FOR CAMPAIGN FINANCE REFORM (%)

	ALL	OCCASIONAL	REGULAR	HABITUAL
PREFERRED REFORMS				
Spending limits	73	81	72	72
Limit TV ads	61	71	62	52
Ban soft money	76	84	75	72
Ban PAC contributions	49	62	46	41
Public funding	38	37	37	39
Free television ads	40	43	38	39
Allow larger individual contributions	37	35	35	42
No limits, disclosure	35	32	34	39
Larger party contributions	28	25	27	30
RESPONSE TO REFORMS				
If ban PACs, would				
Give more	24	23	22	26
Give same	69	69	69	69
Give less	7	8	8	4
If increase individual limit, would				
Give more	18	10	19	24
Give same	78	82	77	75
Give less	5	8	4	2
(*N*)	(946)	(276)	(367)	(303)

Notes: The columns record the percent of individuals who agree or strongly agree with each reform.
Source: The House and Senate Contributor Study.

talking fifty districts. What are you supposed to do in providing all of those people free time?" Yet even those who opposed public financing often told us in personal interviews that they would not rule it out entirely. One conservative donor said: "I oppose public financing on philosophical grounds, but we may have reached the point where we need to consider it." Other donors opposed public financing but thought that it might be part of a larger package of reforms, including spending limits.

Not only have large donors developed strong views about campaign finance reform; they have also given some thought to how they would react if certain reforms were put into place, including a ban on PAC contributions or an increase in the individual contribution limits. Nearly a quarter of respondents in all categories would give more if PACs were banned. In contrast, only 10 percent of occasional donors would give more if individual limits were raised, compared with 24 percent of habitual donors. Clearly, an increase in the contribution limits would increase the share of contributions coming from habitual donors.

THE SOURCES OF ATTITUDES ON REFORM

The campaign contributors who participated in our study are for the most part well informed about campaign finance reform. Many understand the partisan implications of various reforms, doubtlessly because they have been exposed to arguments made by party activists and leaders. Most Republican Party leaders have argued for policies that allow them to use their financial advantages, including raising contribution limits and allowing more party activity, whereas Democratic leaders are more likely to want to limit spending and minimize the financial edge of the GOP. Conservative leaders are less supportive of giving government funds to aid candidates, or imposing mandates on the television industry to provide free advertising. Doubtless the attitudes of large congressional contributors toward reform are rooted in these and other factors.

To learn about the sources of large donors' attitudes toward reforms, we created scales to measure large donors' support for three of the most frequently debated campaign finance proposals: greater limits on spending and contributing, raising or eliminating limits, and public funding.[21] We sought to predict these attitudes with the same demographic variables used in Table 3-5. Instead of strength of partisanship and ideology, we included measures of the direction of these sentiments. We also included measures of the three main motives for giving, and the five decision-making criteria.

The sources of these attitudes are complex and vary by reform proposal (see Table 3-8 on page 64). Occasional donors were more supportive of tighter spending and contribution limits. Jews and liberals were also more likely to support limits, as were those who attended church frequently. Those who make their contribution decisions based on local criteria supported stronger limits, as did those who give to influence a specific issue in Congress. In contrast, those who give because of their involvement in personal networks, or to help advance party candidates, are less likely to support tighter spending limits.

Support for raising contribution limits comes from those with higher levels of education, from Catholics and Jews, from conservatives, and from those with material motives. Support for public funding comes from those with higher levels of education, from those who attend church frequently, from Catholics and secular citizens, from Democrats and liberals, and from those who make contribution decisions based on local criteria. Support is lower among those who decide based on party or ideological criteria.

Taken together, these data show most importantly why campaign finance reform is so difficult to enact in the United States. Democrats and liberals favor limits and public financing, whereas Republicans are more likely to oppose both measures and to support increases in contribution limits. It is important to remember, however, that a majority of Republicans actually oppose raising or eliminating contribution limits—they are merely much more likely than Democrats to support these measures.

TABLE 3-8   THE RELATIVE IMPORTANCE OF DIFFERENT DONOR CHARACTERISTICS
IN THEIR SUPPORT FOR DIFFERENT CAMPAIGN REFORMS

	LIMITS	NO LIMITS	PUBLIC FINANCING
Income	.043	.049	−.003
	(.040)	(.040)	(.036)
Education	.039	−.063**	−.073***
	(.033)	(.033)	(.029)
Female	.073	.029	.054
	(.099)	(.099)	(.088)
Republican	−.013	.088***	−.101***
	(.027)	(.027)	(.024)
Conservative	.082***	−.088***	.153***
	(.035)	(.035)	(.031)
Habitual contributor	.168**	−.037	−.117*
	(.092)	(.092)	(.082)
Occasional contributor	−.206**	−.004	−.171**
	(.094)	(.094)	(.084)
Frequency of church attendance	.081***	.004	−.083***
	(.033)	(.033)	(.029)
Evangelical protestant	−.088	.073	.125
	(.133)	(.134)	(.119)
Catholic	−.03	−.256***	−.264***
	(.103)	(.103)	(.091)
Jewish	−.253**	−.223**	−.181*
	(.129)	(.129)	(.114)
Secular	.064	−.157	−.312**
	(.169)	(.169)	(.150)
Material motive	.011	.095	−.011
	(.043)	(.043)	(.038)
Purposive motive	.041	.010	.016
	(.039)	(.039)	(.035)
Solidary motive	−.008	−.044	.036
	(.040)	(.040)	(.035)
Business criteria	−.021	−.057	.04
	(.046)	(.046)	(.041)
Personal networks	.088**	.045	−.064**
	(.042)	(.042)	(.038)
Party/ideology criteria	.120***	−.029	−.098***
	(.041)	(.041)	(.036)
Local criteria	−.161***	−.007	.102***
	(.038)	(.038)	(.034)
Issue/influence Congress criteria	−.115***	.002	−.042
	(.038)	(.038)	(.034)
Constant	−.916***	.185	.343
	(.378)	(.378)	(.335)
(N)	(703)	(703)	(703)
R^2	.13	.11	.31

Notes: ***$p \leq .01$; **$p \leq .05$; *$p \leq .10$, one tailed tests.
Source: The House and Senate Contributor Study.

Clearly, partisan donors understand the underlying logic of reform. One liberal Democratic woman who was a habitual donor told us she supported spending limits and public financing, but she was less certain about soft money. "Without it, Bob Dole would be president and that troubles me. Dole is not a bad man, it's just that Clinton would not have been competitive just on the small money from his supporters." Another liberal Democratic woman opposed banning PACs because it would give groups like the Christian Coalition an advantage, since the Coalition's church-based distribution of voter guides is not conducted through a PAC.

Beyond the partisan and ideological divide, there are some intriguing differences. Catholics are more likely to oppose relaxing contribution limits and to support public funding than are others who share their ideology and partisanship. Jews were more likely to support both tighter spending limits and laxer contribution limits. These two positions are not contradictory; it is possible to favor relaxing the contribution limits for hard money and political parties, while banning soft money and imposing spending limits. Frequent churchgoers were significantly more likely to favor spending limits and public financing, regardless of the type of church they attended.

The motives and decision-making criteria for giving tell a complicated tale. Those who give because of personal networks are less likely to favor spending limits or public financing. Yet those who give for local reasons are more likely to favor each policy. Clearly, national networks of solicitation, based on complex and sometimes reciprocal relationships, are different from local networks that turn out constituents for a candidate's barbeque. Those who use party and ideology to aid their contribution decisions are less supportive of spending limits or public financing, in part because in our survey these donors tend to be conservative Republicans who perceive a party advantage in unlimited giving.

Yet those who seek to influence specific issues in Congress were more likely to favor contribution and spending limits. Many of these donors give small contributions through the mail, and fear that large donors may have much more impact than they do on policy-making. One ideologically oriented donor who based his contribution decisions on specific issues in Congress favored spending and contribution limits. He noted that these reforms would not affect his giving, since his contributions are small: "Meaningful reform would restrict people who give large amounts to get specific things from the government—a minority of givers but a large proportion of the money."

CONCLUSION

Candidates for House elections must raise large sums of money, and much of this money comes from individual donors. These donors do not "look like America"; they are affluent white older men who are heavily conservative and Republican. Some give habitually in all elections to all types of candidates, some give regularly in most elections to several types of candidates, and some are occasional donors who give to one or two candidates in some campaigns. Donors give for a mix of motives—some to help protect their business or expand its profits, some because of the social benefits or a sense of obligation, and some because they care about the policies of government and the candidates who support them. Habitual donors are more motivated by each of these factors than are occasional donors.

Most donors are asked to give more often than they actually contribute. Contributors decide to whom to give based on five sets of criteria. Some choose based on whether the candidate is friendly to their business, others seek to influence specific policies in Congress, and still others choose candidates from their party who are in close elections. Some contributors' decisions are based not on the candidates but rather on their solicitors, and are embedded in national or local networks.

Perhaps the most surprising finding is the strong support for campaign finance reform among donors. Large majorities think the system needs major reform, and feel increasing pressure from candidates to give larger and larger amounts. There is broad-based support for limits to spending and a ban on soft money, but less support for either raising contribution limits or public funding. There are partisan and ideological divisions among donors about precisely which reforms they support, reflecting their sophisticated understanding of the campaign finance system. Donors understand the connection between public funding and spending limits, but many believe that candidates and parties would circumvent any new limits regardless of whether their campaigns were subsidized. Donors believe that giving is legitimate and they enjoy contributing to candidates whom they support, but a majority of donors believe that the system has gotten out of control. Whether incumbents can respond effectively to the donors who support their campaigns, however, remains to be seen.

APPENDIX A: THE HOUSE AND SENATE CONTRIBUTOR STUDY

The questionnaire was mailed to individuals who contributed $200 or more to one or more candidates competing in the 1996 congressional elections. The first wave of the survey was mailed in August 1997. Two follow-ups were sent to individuals who did not respond to the earlier mailings. The response rate was 50 percent, excluding undeliverable questionnaires. A report on the survey can be found at http//:www.georgetown.edu/wilcox/donors.htm.

APPENDIX B: OPERATIONALIZATION OF THE VARIABLES

Income is coded 1 for a family income less than $50,000, 2 for a family income between $50,000 and $99,000, 3 for a family income between $100,000 and $249,000, 4 for a family income between $250,000 and $500,000, and 5 for a family income $500,000 and more.

Education is coded 1 for high school or less, 2 for some college, 3 for college graduate, 4 for some graduate school, and 5 for graduate degree.

Gender is coded 1 for male and 2 for female.

Frequency of Church Attendance is coded 1 for more than once a week, 2 for once a week, 3 for several times a month, 4 for a few times a year, and 5 for seldom or never.

The religious denomination variables are a series of separate variables, each coded as 1 if the respondent fits into the specific category. These categories are *Evangelical Protestant*, *Catholic*, *Jewish*, and *Secular*.

Strength of Partisanship is measured using a 7-point scale with 1 representing strong Republican, 4 representing Independent, and 7 representing strong Democrat.

Political Ideology is measured using a 7-point scale with 1 representing extremely liberal, 4 representing moderate, and 7 representing extremely conservative.

Group Attachment is a count of the number of types of groups to which each respondent belonged.

Donors are defined as *Habitual contributors* if they give regularly to candidates at all level of government. They are *Occasional contributors* if they give only in some elections to a few types of candidates. *Regular contributors* give in most elections to several types of candidates.

Material Motives, *Purposive Motives*, and *Solidary Motives* are measured by a factor score, with high scores representing stronger motives.

Business Criteria are measured by a factor score, comprised primarily of criteria relating to business and employment. *Personal Networks Criteria* are measured by a factor score, comprised primarily of criteria relating to personal relationships between those who asked for the money and those who gave it. *Party/Ideological Criteria* are measured by a factor score, comprised primarily of criteria relating to helping candidates with a particular partisan or ideological profile and those in close elections. *Local Criteria* are measured by a factor score, comprised primarily of criteria relating to local political conditions and friendship with candidates. *Issue/Influence Congress Criteria* are measured by a factor score, comprised primarily of criteria relating to influencing the policy outputs of Congress or of a particular committee. High scores represent stronger influence.

Solicitations is an estimate of the number of House and Senate candidates who asked the respondent to give in the 1996 elections.

ACKNOWLEDGMENT

The research for this chapter was supported by a grant from the Joyce Foundation. The opinions expressed in this chapter are those of the authors and do not necessarily reflect the views of the Joyce Foundation.

NOTES

1. Frank J. Sorauf, *Inside Campaign Finance: Myths and Realities* (New Haven: Yale University Press, 1992), 9–12; John R. Wright, *Interest Groups & Congress: Lobbying, Contributions, and Influence* (Boston, MA: Allyn & Bacon, 1996), 121; Mark J. Rozell and Clyde Wilcox, *Interest Groups in American Campaigns* (Washington, DC: CQ Press, 1999), 75–76; Paul S. Herrnson, *Congressional Elections: Campaigning at Home and in Washington*, 3rd ed. (Washington, DC: CQ Press, 2000), 269–272.
2. Diana Dwyre, "Spinning Straw into Gold: Soft Money and U.S. House Elections," *Legislative Studies Quarterly* 21 (1996): 411; James A. Barnes, "New Rules for the Money Game," *National Journal*, July 6, 1996.
3. Clyde Wilcox, "I Owe It All to Me: Candidates' Investments in Their Own Campaigns," *American Politics Quarterly* 16 (1988): 266–279; Robert Biersack, Paul S. Herrnson, and Clyde Wilcox, "Seeds for Success: Early Money in Congressional Elections," *Legislative Studies Quarterly* 18 (1993): 535–552.
4. Herrnson, *Congressional Elections*, 154–163.
5. Richard F. Fenno Jr., *Home Style: House Members in Their Districts* (Boston: Little, Brown, 1978), 164–168.
6. The figures are for 1999; Roger H. Davidson and Walter J. Oleszek, *Congress and Its Members*, 7th ed. (Washington, DC: CQ Press, 2000), 154.
7. There is some debate among academics about whether war chests do in fact deter challengers. See Jonathan S. Krasno and Donald Phillip Green, "Preempting Quality Challengers in House Elections," *Journal of Politics* 50 (1988), 920–936; and Janet M. Box-Steffensmeier, "A Dynamic Analysis of the Role of War Chests in Campaign Strategy," *American Journal of Political Science* 40 (1996): 352–371.
8. Competitive races are defined as contested elections decided by 20 percent or less of the two-party vote.
9. See Robert Biersack, Paul S. Herrnson, and Clyde Wilcox, eds., *Risky Business? PAC Decisionmaking in Congressional Elections* (Armonk, NY: M. E. Sharpe, 1994); Robert Biersack, Paul S. Herrnson, and Clyde Wilcox, *After the Revolution: PACS, Lobbies, and the Republican Congress* (Boston: Allyn & Bacon, 1999).
10. Herrnson, *Congressional Elections*, 160–161.
11. Center for Responsive Politics, http://www.opensecrets.org/politicians/geog/H6NC04037.htm.
12. Biersack, Herrnson, and Wilcox, *Risky Business?*, 535–552.
13. Wilcox, "I Owe It All to Me," 266–279.
14. Herrnson, *Congressional Elections*, 169–170.
15. Robert S. Biersack, John C. Green, Paul S. Herrnson, Lynda Powell, and Clyde Wilcox, *The Financiers of Congressional Elections: Investors, Ideologues, and Intimates* (in press).
16. This estimate for the amount that was contributed was calculated from a question that asked how many contributions to House candidates each contributor had made within specific ranges of amounts. We simply took the midpoint of the range, and multiplied it by the number of contributions. Thus if a respondent claimed 2 contributions of amounts between $750 and $1,000, we estimated their total contributions as 2 x $875.

17. John C. Green, Paul S. Herrnson, Lynda Powell, and Clyde Wilcox, "Women Big Donors Mobilized in Congressional Elections," http://www.bsos.umd.edu/gvpt/herrnson/women.html.
18. Barbara Levick-Segnatelli, "The Washington PAC: One Man Can Make a Difference," in Robert Biersack, Paul S. Herrnson, and Clyde Wilcox, eds., *Risky Business: PAC Decisionmaking in Congressional Elections* (Armonk, NY: M. E. Sharpe, 1994), 202–213; Clifford W. Brown Jr., Lynda W. Powell, and Clyde Wilcox, *Serious Money: Fundraising and Contributing in Presidential Nomination Campaigns* (New York: Cambridge University Press, 1995), 119; Clyde Wilcox, *Onward Christian Soldiers: The Christian Right in American Politics*, 2nd ed. (Boulder, CO: Westview Press, forthcoming in 2000).
19. This interpretation is based on the results from a regression equation that was identical to the one in Table 3-5, column 2, except that it excluded a variable for the number of solicitations. The relationship between gender and contributions was not statistically significant in this equation.
20. This interpretation is based on the results from a regression equation that was identical to the one in Table 3-5, column 2, except that it excluded a variable for the number of solicitations. The relationships between being an Evangelical Protestant, a Jew, or a secular donor and contributions were significant in this equation.
21. These scales are factor scores from a factor analysis of all reform proposals.

4

Are Professional Campaigns More Negative?

OWEN G. ABBE / PAUL S. HERRNSON
DAVID B. MAGLEBY / KELLY D. PATTERSON

In recent years political observers have voiced concerns over the negative tone of campaigns and the professionalism of their staffing. These two trends have raised concerns among political scientists and observers of politics. Those who are primarily concerned with negative advertising believe that attack ads contribute to greater voter cynicism, lower voter turnout, and a general decline in the civility of American politics. Those who are uneasy about increases in campaign professionalism blame consultants for rising campaign costs and the declining importance of volunteers. They are also concerned that consultants usurp many campaign functions formerly carried out by political parties and emphasize tactics designed solely to win elections rather than to elect effective officeholders.

The coincidence of these two trends raises important questions. Has the rise of political consultants contributed to the increased negativity of political campaigns? Are more professionally run campaigns more negative than those waged by amateurs? We investigate the latter question using a new data set that combines campaign finance figures and election returns with campaign information collected from candidates and campaign aides who competed in the 1998 House races. We find that professional campaigns are significantly more prone to attack their opponents, but that contrary to received opinion, negative campaigning is no more effective than positive campaigning.

CAMPAIGN PROFESSIONALISM AND NEGATIVE CAMPAIGNING

Negative campaigning is not a new practice by any stretch of the imagination, but sophisticated techniques have transformed the mudslinging of former years.[1] Informed by polls and demographic targeting and fueled by opposition research, negative messages are carefully calculated to peel away the opponent's support among specific groups. This "new style" of campaigning exploits mass marketing tools, such as television advertising, direct mail, automated phone banks, demographic targeting, and scientific polling.[2]

The old style of campaigning relied on party organizations whereby politicians secured party nominations and general election votes by forming alliances with ward politicians, who controlled votes by providing services such as jobs, contracts, protection from the law, and welfare assistance. The new techniques required to reach the mass electorate involve a different kind of expertise.[3] The intricacies of ad design and production, survey research, and media relations depart from the patronage and interpersonal skills of party machine politics. Where party operatives once dominated campaign organizations, now a diversified cadre of consultants deliver candidate messages to voters.[4] The tasks of managing the campaign, designing media advertising, conducting polls, performing opposition research, and raising campaign funds all require specialized skills for optimum efficiency.

Campaign professionals' beliefs about strategies and tactics are central to how campaigns are conducted. For example, consultants almost universally agree that negative ads are effective, leading them to encourage candidates to go negative.[5] A recent survey showed that 80 percent of campaign consultants claimed responsibility for the decision to attack an opponent's personal character or record.[6] Not surprisingly, the new style campaign is usually both professional and negative.

DATA AND METHODS

We systematically assess the degree to which more professional campaigns are more negative in tone, using data collected from a survey of candidates and campaign aides who competed in major-party contested House races during the 1998 general elections and campaign finance data provided by the Federal Election Commission (FEC). The survey collected information on negative advertising, campaign organizations, political strategies and tactics, and campaign budgets. The response rate was 44 percent and the sample is representative of the underlying population of House general election campaigns (see Appendix A for more information about this survey). We use logistic regression analysis to estimate the impact of campaign professionals on the likelihood that a campaign will use negative advertisements and ordinary least squares regression analysis to estimate the influence that professionals and negative ads have on electoral performance. Case studies drawn from the 1998 elections are used to illustrate the findings.

CAMPAIGN PROFESSIONALISM

Modern campaigns involve a range of activities such as campaign management, media advertising, press relations, issue and opposition research, polling, fund-raising, get-out-the-vote drives, legal advice, and accounting or filing of FEC reports. Congressional candidates rely on a variety of staff resources to carry out these activities. Paid campaign staff, paid consultants, party staff, union members, unpaid volunteers, and members of supporting groups may all participate in a candidate's campaign. Paid campaign staffers and paid consultants are campaign professionals. They are distinct from others who work on campaigns in two ways: First, they have the experience and skills necessary to mount a successful campaign. Most consultants develop valuable skills such as polling, designing direct mail, or producing television ads in college, working for a political party, or working in the marketing and advertising industries. They spend several years with a political consulting firm before striking out on their own. Second, professionals are paid by candidates to apply their expertise in the candidate's behalf. Their goal is to make sure the candidate footing the bill runs as well as possible. Volunteers, party staff, and members of supporting groups often have their own agendas in working with the candidate, including promoting specific public policies. Professionals can provide valuable services in each of nine major campaign activities: campaign management, media advertising, press relations, issue and opposition research, polling, fund-raising, get-out-the-vote drives, legal advice, and accounting or filing of FEC reports.

Campaign management involves the formation, implementation, and coordination of a coherent campaign strategy and orchestrating the activities of political consultants and campaign staff.[7] Professional campaign managers also bring experience and strategic insights that may be lacked by candidates. Candidates who are political amateurs have little experience with campaigning, and incumbents must spend time governing rather than managing the details of the campaign.

Campaign management is so important that approximately three-quarters of incumbents and open-seat contestants employ a professional manager (see Table 4-1). Challengers lag far behind other candidates in their ability to retain a professional manager, usually because they are short of cash. Nearly one-tenth of all challengers cope without a campaign manager, overseeing their own bids for office. Less than 1 percent of incumbents, and no open-seat contestants, went without a campaign manager.

Campaigns use a variety of mass media, including radio and direct mail, to communicate their theme or message to voters, but television typically reaches the widest audience. It also requires the greatest skill to exploit effectively. Regardless of the medium, campaigns that employ political professionals

TABLE 4-1   THE TYPE OF STAFF PERFORMING CAMPAIGN ACTIVITIES (%)

	ALL	INCUMBENTS	CHALLENGERS	OPEN SEATS
Campaign Management				
Campaign staff	59.9	70.8	46.3	78.1
Paid consultant	15.5	16.9	15.0	12.5
Party staff	2.3	.8	3.4	3.1
Union members	—	—	—	—
Unpaid volunteers	21.0	11.5	3.3	12.5
Other groups	2.3	3.1	2.0	—
Not used	4.5	.8	8.8	—
Media Advertising				
Campaign staff	18.7	19.8	18.4	15.6
Paid consultant	55.2	68.7	40.8	65.6
Party staff	1.3	1.5	.7	3.1
Union members	—	—	—	—
Unpaid volunteers	12.6	.8	23.1	12.5
Other groups	4.5	3.8	5.4	3.1
Not used	11.3	9.2	15.0	3.1
Press Relations				
Campaign staff	57.0	67.7	44.9	68.8
Paid consultant	15.5	16.9	12.9	21.9
Party staff	2.9	2.3	4.1	—
Union members	—	—	—	—
Unpaid volunteers	19.7	8.5	30.6	15.6
Other groups	3.2	3.1	4.1	—
Not used	6.1	3.1	10.2	—
Issue and Opposition Research				
Campaign staff	33.4	43.1	27.2	22.6
Paid consultant	28.6	32.3	19.0	58.1
Party staff	8.1	3.8	12.9	3.2
Union members	.3	—	—	3.2
Unpaid volunteers	18.8	6.9	31.3	9.7
Other groups	5.2	3.1	6.8	6.5
Not used	11.7	14.6	11.6	—
Polling				
Campaign staff	5.5	6.9	4.1	6.3
Paid consultant	55.8	67.2	40.8	78.1
Party staff	2.9	3.1	2.7	3.1
Union members	.3	—	.7	—
Unpaid volunteers	8.7	3.8	15.0	—
Other groups	1.6	1.5	2.0	—
Not used	28.1	20.6	38.1	12.5

TABLE 4-1 (CONT.)

	ALL	INCUMBENTS	CHALLENGERS	OPEN SEATS
Fund-raising				
Campaign staff	58.9	65.6	49.3	75.0
Paid consultant	21.4	28.2	11.0	40.6
Party staff	4.2	3.8	4.1	6.3
Union members	1.0	.8	.7	3.1
Unpaid volunteers	19.7	12.2	27.4	15.6
Other groups	2.6	1.5	4.1	—
Not used	5.8	—	12.3	—
Get-Out-the-Vote				
Campaign staff	27.4	32.1	17.0	56.3
Paid consultant	10.0	9.9	10.2	9.4
Party staff	22.9	25.2	22.4	15.6
Union members	6.5	9.2	4.8	3.1
Unpaid volunteers	50.3	48.1	49.0	65.6
Other groups	4.2	3.8	4.1	6.3
Not used	9.0	4.6	14.3	—
Legal Advice				
Campaign staff	9.8	14.1	6.8	6.3
Paid consultant	21.9	31.3	13.7	21.9
Party staff	11.4	9.4	12.3	15.6
Union members	—	—	—	—
Unpaid volunteers	30.1	19.5	39.7	28.1
Other groups	6.9	5.5	7.5	9.4
Not used	24.2	21.9	26.7	21.9
Accounting/Filing FEC Reports				
Campaign staff	45.2	63.4	29.9	40.6
Paid consultant	16.8	24.4	8.8	21.9
Party staff	2.6	2.3	3.4	—
Union members	—	—	—	—
Unpaid volunteers	31.9	11.5	48.3	40.6
Other groups	2.9	1.5	4.8	—
Not used	4.5	.8	8.8	—
Professionalism Index	5.30	6.57	3.93	6.38
(*N*)	(313)	(132)	(149)	(32)

to develop their advertisements are usually at an advantage. Candidates differ in experience, qualifications, and issue stances. The major challenge for campaigners lies in persuading voters which differences in a given election matter and which differences should be ignored. Well-designed ads can increase the candidate's name identification, project an appealing image of the candidate, and develop or exploit voters' issue awareness in ways help-ful to the candidate.[8] About one-fifth of all House campaigns have adver-tising experts on staff to help them shape their election communications. Most candidates retain independent media consultants, although many chal-lengers have difficulty affording media consultants. Roughly one-quarter rely solely on volunteers and another 15 percent make do without any media advice.

Many candidates believe that election news coverage, often referred to as "earned" or "free" media, is just as critical to a campaign as paid adver-tising. News coverage can be obtained with minimal cost and is more cred-ible than paid advertisements. However, unlike paid advertising, a campaign cannot control the content of news reports. To help generate and direct free press coverage, almost all campaigns try to cultivate positive relationships with journalists. Campaigns issue press releases, invite the media to signif-icant campaign events, and answer reporters' inquiries. Most campaigns use paid staff members to coordinate media. Incumbents often hire the press secretary from their congressional office, who takes a leave of absence from normal duties to fulfill this role. Open-seat contestants use more consultants than either incumbents or challengers. More than 30 percent of all chal-lengers rely on volunteers for their press relations.

Issue and opposition research serves three functions in a campaign. First, it helps candidates develop issue positions related to their campaign mes-sage. Second, it provides candidates with ammunition with which to criti-cize the opponent. Third, it prepares a candidate for potential attacks by an opponent. Different types of campaigns rely on different resources to per-form issue and opposition research. Incumbents are the most inclined to use paid staff members for this function. Open-seat contestants rely principally on paid consultants, while challengers again turn to volunteers.

Polling provides candidates with information on voters' attitudes. In the early stages of a campaign, this information is critical in shaping cam-paign messages. Polls also allow a candidate to monitor how the voters are responding to campaign messages once advertising begins. Like media ad-vertising, polling requires highly specialized skills and is quite expensive. Paid consultants are essentially synonymous with polling because amateur polls are rarely accurate enough to be reliable. Most incumbents commis-sion polls, but nearly 21 percent—usually those who face weak challengers—do not. Thirty-eight percent of all challengers forgo polls, usually because they cannot afford them. Open-seat candidates are the least likely to cam-paign without commissioning polls.

Fund-raising provides the lifeblood of campaigning. A campaign can-not hire staff, commission polls, or buy ads without money. Fund-raising is a diverse activity that involves direct mail, telemarketing, personal visits from the candidate or campaign staff, large receptions or dinners featuring prominent guests, intimate functions that offer more direct access to the candidate, and even the Internet. Most campaigns rely on paid staff members to keep contributions flowing. Open-seat candidates are much more likely to have paid staff or consultants raising money for them. Challengers are the most likely to do without professional fund-raising assistance.

Voter mobilization, unlike most other campaign activities, requires fewer specialists but more workers. Only about one-tenth of campaigns involve professional consultants in voter registration and get-out-the-vote efforts. Unpaid volunteers dominate the field of voter mobilization, but campaign and party staff also play an important role. Over one-half of all open-seat and nearly one-third of all incumbent candidates use paid campaign staff to mobilize voters, as opposed to 17 percent of all challengers.

Legal advice and accounting are less visible aspects of campaigning but are extremely important elements of contemporary House campaigns. Most campaigns need little legal advice and can get what they need through informal consultation. Almost one-third of all campaigns rely on lawyers who provide their expertise on a volunteer basis. Some campaigns, usually those waged by incumbents and open-seat contestants, face more complex issues. They may turn to party officials for advice or hire outside legal expertise. Still, many campaigns are able to do without any legal services at all.

Incumbent, challenger, and open-seat campaigns handle accounting and filing FEC disclosure reports differently. Because many incumbents have perpetual campaign organizations and are constantly raising money, they have a permanent accountant or consultant to handle their financial records. Challengers rely primarily on volunteers. Open-seat candidates are evenly divided between using campaign staff and volunteers for accounting and submitting FEC reports.

In general, most modern House candidates assemble professional campaign organizations. The index of campaign professionalism at the bottom of Table 4-1 is the average number of campaign activities performed by political consultants or paid staff, ranging from 0 to 9. Incumbents and open-seat candidates use campaign professionals for between 6 and 7 campaign activities. Democrat Tammy Baldwin, the victorious candidate in Wisconsin's 2nd congressional district, for example, fielded a highly professional campaign organization that is characteristic of competitive open-seat races. Paul Devlin, a veteran campaigner, managed her campaign. Baldwin hired seven other full-time staff members to handle press relations, organize fund-raising, and supervise her army of 3,000 volunteers. She also employed the services of several national consulting firms. The Feldman Group of Washington, DC, conducted polls. Will Robinson of McWilliams, Cosgrove, Smith, and Robinson, also of Washington, handled media advertising and general consulting services. Terris and Jaye of San Francisco carried out direct mail. The Tyson Organization provided phone banks in support of the campaign's get-out-the-vote effort.[9]

The data indicate that incumbents run very professional campaigns. This is particularly the case if the incumbent is vulnerable. For example, Rick Hill, a Republican first-term incumbent in Montana's at-large district, relied extensively on professionals in his campaign. Shane Hedges took a leave of absence from Hill's Washington office to manage the campaign and handle press relations. The campaign employed five national consulting firms to provide campaign services. They hired Scott Howl and Company of Dallas, Texas, for media advising; Terry Cooper Political Research of Arlington, Virginia, for issue and opposition research; Bob Moore Information of Portland, Oregon, for polling; Townsend of Alexandria, Virginia, for fund-raising; and Arena Communications of Salt Lake City, Utah, for direct mail. A professional accountant from Helena, Montana, provided accounting services and filed FEC reports. Hill's campaign organization helped carry him to victory with 52 percent of the vote.

Challengers run less professional campaigns, with an average of about 4 campaign activities performed by professionals. Democrat Asuncion "Ceccy" R. Groom, who ran against three-term incumbent Ed Royce in California's Republican-dominated 39th district, assembled a campaign team that was both underfunded and understaffed. Her campaign was originally run by a paid but inexperienced manager. She had difficulty retaining managers and took over the role herself after going through three managers. Groom hired the American Mutual Admiration Company of Redondo Beach for strategic advice. The company also helped her modify generic ads produced by the Democratic Congressional Campaign Committee. Groom relied primarily on volunteers for most of her campaign activities. Personal friends, Democratic activists, and other volunteers provided fund-raising, direct mail, press relations, research, and voter mobilization support. She lost to Royce by 29 percentage points.[10]

NEGATIVE CAMPAIGNING

Negative advertising is prevalent in House campaigns. Both candidates refrained from attacking each other in only 44 percent of all 1998 House races (see Table 4-2 on page 78).[11] Candidates reported that at least one contestant used negative advertising in about 56 percent of House races. Both candidates attacked each other in 20 percent of these contests. Incumbents are the least likely to use negative ads. About 17 percent of incumbents reported using negative ads, as compared to 28 percent of challengers and 41 percent of open-seat candidates.[12] These are conservative estimates because they rely on campaigners' evaluations of their own campaigns. Candidates have a tendency to underestimate the negativity of

Table 4-2   Campaigners' Perceptions of Who Used Negative Advertising (%)

	All	Incumbents	Challengers	Open Seats
Candidate only	4.5	.8	7.4	6.3
Opponent only	31.6	42.4	22.1	31.3
Both candidate and opponent	20.1	16.7	20.1	34.4
Neither candidate nor opponent	43.8	40.2	50.3	28.1
(N)	(313)	(132)	(149)	(32)

their own communications and overestimate the negativity of the messages disseminated by their opponents.

Negative advertising can take place through just about any means of mass communication, including billboards, mail, newsprint, phone banks, radio, and television. The most popular media for attacks are direct mail (because of its capacity for precise targeting) and television (because of its ability to reach the widest possible audience with compelling images). An example of negative direct-mail advertising occurred in California's 46th district, where Republican Bob Dornan used targeted attack mailers to try to undermine support for incumbent Loretta Sanchez among Catholic Hispanics. The cover of the mailer presented the image of the Blessed Mother. Inside the mailer were diagrams detailing the partial-birth abortion procedure and a picture of Sanchez.[13] The attack capitalized on Orange County bishop Norman F. McFarland's criticism of Sanchez for campaigning in Catholic churches while supporting abortion rights.[14] In spite of these attacks, Sanchez won reelection with 56 percent of the vote to Dornan's 39 percent. An example of negative television advertising cropped up in Pennsylvania's 14th district. Here the unsuccessful Republican challenger, William Ravotti, used clever television attacks against Democratic incumbent Bill Coyne. One of Ravotti's ads featured a talking duck who tries to defend Coyne against angry voters:

> How many of you are angry about Coyne voting for the six biggest tax increases in history? How many are upset about Coyne giving himself over $70,000 in pay raises? But look, Coyne has written some very important legislation. Well, OK, in 18 years as our congressman he's only written one bill. But it's a biggie. Thanks to Coyne, we renamed the aviary. Now tell me that ain't worth a $2 million pension.[15]

Are campaign professionals responsible for the high degree of negativity in House races? The answer is clearly yes. Campaign professionalism has a major impact on the decision to attack an opponent. A fully professional campaign that employs political professionals to perform all nine major campaign activities is 19 percent more likely to go negative than is a campaign waged with an entirely amateur organization (see Table 4-3).[16]

TABLE 4-3 THE IMPACT OF CAMPAIGN PROFESSIONALISM
ON THE USE OF NEGATIVE ADVERTISING

	LOGISTIC REGRESSION COEFFICIENT	STANDARD ERROR	CHANGE IN PROBABILITY OF USING NEGATIVE ADS[a] (%)
Campaign professionalism	.15*	.07	19
Challenger	1.11**	.43	17
Open seat	1.03*	.54	19
Party bias	−.002	.008	—
Opponent used negative ads	1.46***	.39	21
Electoral competitiveness	.20	.32	—
Campaign communications spending[b]	−.0003	.0004	—
Opponents campaign Communications spending[b]	.0008*	.0004	72
Independent expenditures[b]	.0098*	.0058	8
Constant	−3.97***	.61	
Cox & Snell R^2 = .219			
Nagelkerke R^2 = .324			
Cases predicted correctly: 82%			
N = 287			

Notes: Results were estimated using logistic regression. The dependent variable is the use of negative advertising.

[a]The change in probability of going negative is calculated by subtracting the probability of going negative at the maximum value of the featured variable from the probability of going negative at the lowest value of the featured variable while holding all other variables constant at their mean value.

[b]These variables are measured in thousands of dollars.

*$p < .05$, **$p < .01$, and ***$p < .001$, using a one-tailed test of significance.

Other factors contribute to the likelihood that a campaign will use negative advertising. Challengers and open-seat candidates are more likely to use negative ads than are incumbents. Because incumbents enjoy many advantages over challengers, such as name recognition, the franking privilege, and disproportionate financial support from access-oriented political action committees, they are usually under less pressure to use negative ads. Challengers, on the other hand, need to give voters a reason to change their previous pro-incumbent voting habits. Consequently, pointing out an incumbent's personal weaknesses, political mistakes, or differences of opinion with constituents becomes an attractive campaign strategy. Moreover, a big part of a challenger's role as a candidate is to hold the incumbent accountable for his or her job performance. As a result, challengers are 17 percent more likely to use negative ads than incumbents. Open-seat candidates are 19 percent more likely to go negative than incumbents. Open-seat candidates are usually engaged in extremely competitive races where voters are not well acquainted with either candidate. Open-seat candidates often take advantage of this unfamiliarity by painting an unfavorable image of their opponent in their advertising.

Maryland's 8th congressional district provides a good example of how incumbent advantages often force challengers to resort to negative strategies. Connie Morella, a moderate Republican, had been reelected five times by substantial margins prior to 1998 in a predominantly Democratic, suburban Washington district. Her challenger, Democrat Ralph Neas, had strong credentials as a civil rights leader but had never held elective office. As a challenger attempting to unseat an entrenched incumbent, he needed to persuade voters not to reelect Morella. To do this, Neas developed a principally negative campaign strategy. His central message was that the Republican Party's conservative agenda did not effectively represent the voters of the 8th district. Neas tried to make the case that Morella's vote for the impeachment investigation of President Clinton provided evidence that she shared her party's conservative views. Neas attacked Morella's impeachment inquiry vote over the radio and aired negative television spots on the same issue in late October. In one television ad, Neas asked voters the following questions:

> What do you want Congress and the president to do for you, for our nation, in the next year? Do you want them working to improve our schools, health care and the environment? Or do you want them mired in the details of Lewinsky, Tripp and Starr? I'm Ralph Neas, a Democrat running for Congress. My opponent, Representative Morella, voted for an open-ended impeachment inquiry. I favor censuring the president, but then getting on with the business of government. The facts don't justify an impeachment. And, we can't afford a government in paralysis.[17]

While Neas's ads attracted national attention for making impeachment a campaign issue, the ads were not successful in eroding Morella's support. She defeated Neas by a 21 percent vote margin.

Not all candidates who go negative make attacking an opponent a central part of their campaign strategy. Some candidates blast their opponent because they think the opponent has given them no option. Jay Bryant, a communications consultant and former director of communications for the National Republican Congressional Committee (NRCC), explains that serious attacks almost always require a candidate to mount a defense in the same medium and of the same magnitude as the attack.[18] Responses can be delivered in the form of a denial, explanation, or apology, but these are not always available and they are usually not as effective as making a counterattack. Some campaigns that are engaged in very competitive races or facing an opponent with a history of attack advertising even prepare responses in advance so they can respond immediately to expected attacks. Candidates who believe that their opponent has attacked them are 21 percent more likely to use negative ads themselves.

The race in Massachusetts's 6th congressional district illustrates this pattern. The contest was the third match between Democratic incumbent John Tierney and Republican challenger Peter Torkildsen. Torkildsen had previously represented the district in Congress for two terms before Tierney unseated him in 1996 by a paper-thin margin of only 360 votes. In 1998 Torkildsen sought to retake the seat. Democratic voters outnumber Republicans in the 6th district, but the presence of many independent voters makes the district competitive.[19]

Tierney's initial strategy emphasized his accomplishments in office, but his campaign changed the tone of its messages in reply to attacks by Torkildsen. Torkildsen criticized Tierney for losing defense dollars for the district by turning down a seat on the House National Security Committee. He also criticized Tierney as being ineffective on education and Social Security, Tierney's primary campaign issues from his 1996 campaign. Tierney responded by criticizing Torkildsen's record from his days in Congress and associating Torkildsen with Republican House leader Newt Gingrich, who was unpopular with Massachusetts voters. In the end, Tierney held his seat with 54 percent of the vote.[20]

Campaigns are also more likely to resort to attack advertising when facing a well-financed opponent. The typical challenger spent $160,000 on campaign communications and had a 42 percent probability of attacking the incumbent. The typical incumbent spent roughly $360,000 and had a probability of 16 percent of attacking the challenger. Candidates in higher-spending contests, which tend to be more competitive, are even more likely to attack their opponent. A challenger like Torkildsen, who spent an estimated $520,000 on campaign communications, had a 61 percent probability of attacking the incumbent. An incumbent like Tierney, who spent an estimated $630,000 on campaign communications, had a 33 percent probability of responding in kind.

When parties and interest groups mount independent expenditure campaigns to influence an election, this increases the likelihood that a campaign will use negative advertising. Individuals and groups may seek to influence the outcome of an election independent of candidates' own campaigns by making independent expenditures on communications that advocate the election or defeat of a candidate—expenditures that must be reported to the FEC—or by using issue advocacy messages that do not expressly call for the election or defeat of a candidate and thus are not subject to disclosure laws. These independent efforts to influence elections tend to be more negative than candidates' own campaigns.[21]

When independent groups become involved, candidates can lose the ability to control both the substance and the tone of campaign messages. Candidates who use negative ads run the risk of alienating voters; some voters respond to mean-spirited attacks by voting against the candidate responsible for the ads. Independent groups, on the other hand, rarely have to worry much about backlash effects because they often fail to identify themselves or they use cryptic names like America First or Citizens for Better Government. More important, unlike the candidates, their names do not appear on the ballot because they are not up for election.

When independent groups make unfair attacks against a candidate, voters have difficulty knowing whom to hold responsible. Once independent groups use negative messages, candidates may find it necessary to escalate the rhetoric of their own campaigns. Interest-group attacks were common in the 1998 elections, particularly in hotly contested races. In Pennsylvania, the AFL-CIO did push-polling—a telephone call used to communicate negative information rather than measure public opinion—for Patrick Casey, a Democrat running against Don Sherwood for an open seat.[22] In Massachusetts' 6th district, the NRCC ran negative ads against Tierney under the pseudonym "Citizens for Better Government."[23] When candidates face independent groups opposing their election, they may be as much as 8 percent more likely to use negative ads.

NEGATIVE ADVERTISING, CAMPAIGN PROFESSIONALISM, AND ELECTORAL SUCCESS

Modern campaigns use political professionals and negative advertising because candidates and consultants believe that these resources win elections. Are these beliefs justified? After controlling for other relevant factors, do professional campaigns and campaigns that air negative ads perform better at the polls? We find that candidates with professional campaigns reap electoral gains. A candidate receives roughly 0.7 percent more of the vote for each campaign activity that is performed by a professional (see Table 4-4). A candidate who had professionals conducting all nine campaign activities typically received just over 6 percent more of the vote than a campaign that had professionals performing none of them. Candidates who assembled more typical campaigns—ones that employed professionals to perform seven campaign activities—against opponents who employed professionals to carry out three campaign activities garnered on average 3 percent more of the vote.

Counter to the conventional wisdom among political consultants, we find that negative campaigns do no better at the polls than positive campaigns. This finding does not mean that negative ads never play a role in determining the outcome of an election. Indeed, the broad-brush strokes of systematic research sometimes mask specific instances where negative ads do matter. In some cases individual negative ads that accurately and effectively criticize an opponent's record can detract from that candidate's ability to win swing votes or discourage the candidate's supporters from turning out to vote.[24] The campaign waged by Democratic challenger Rush Holt effectively used negative ads to demonstrate that Republican incumbent Mike Pappas was out of

TABLE 4-4   THE IMPACT OF CAMPAIGN PROFESSIONALISM
AND NEGATIVE ADVERTISING ON THE CANDIDATE'S VOTE SHARE

	REGRESSION COEFFICIENT	STANDARD ERROR
Campaign professionalism	.684***	.18
Candidate used negative ads	−.73	1.08
Opponent used negative ads	.32	.97
Challenger	−12.99***	1.89
Open seat	−3.5*	1.86
Party bias	.20***	.02
Political experience	2.80***	.69
Media advantage	4.29***	1.05
Campaign communications spending[a]	−.0002	.001
Opponent's campaign communications spending[a]	−.0010	.001
Independent expenditures[a]	−.018	.013
Constant	41.82***	2.94
$R^2 = .817$		
$N = 287$		

Notes: Results were estimated using ordinary least squares regression. The dependent variable is the candidate's vote share in the general election.

[a]These variables are measured in thousands of dollars.

$*p < .05$, $**p < .01$, and $***p < .001$, using a one-tailed test of significance.

touch with the moderate voters of New Jersey's 12th district. Holt ran several ads featuring Pappas singing a poem to the tune of "Twinkle, Twinkle, Little Star" on the House floor to commemorate Kenneth Starr's birthday:

> MICHAEL PAPPAS: Twinkle, Twinkle, Kenneth Starr. Now we see how brave you are …
> ANNOUNCER: That's Congressman Michael Pappas.
> MICHAEL PAPPAS: We could not see which way to go, if you did not lead us so …
> ANNOUNCER: Congressman Pappas opposes the assault weapons ban. Voted against smaller class sizes. Voted with insurance companies over patients.
> MICHAEL PAPPAS: Twinkle, Twinkle all brought down. Twinkle Twinkle Kenneth Starr …
> ANNOUNCER: Partisan investigations instead of real work. Congressman Michael Pappas: Out of tune. Out of touch.[25]

The ad helped Holt receive a cross-party endorsement from Tom Kean, a popular Republican former governor of New Jersey.[26] Holt ultimately went on to defeat the incumbent with 51 percent of the vote to Pappas's 48 percent.

Negative campaigning also appears to have helped Democrat Tammy Baldwin win an open-seat contest in Wisconsin's 2nd district. Baldwin took advantage of her Republican opponent Jo Musser's slow start to neutralize one of Musser's potential strengths. As a former insurance commissioner for the state of Wisconsin, Musser had a sound understanding of health care issues and good working relations with insurers. However, while Musser's campaign was still recovering from a divisive primary battle, Baldwin launched an ad campaign that implied that Musser had been a tool of the insurance industry and highlighted Musser's contributions from insurance PACs. Baldwin went on to win with a 7 percent margin over Musser.[27]

Negative campaigning can also backfire and cause greater harm than good to the candidate who makes the attack when negative information is misleading, unconvincing, or subject to harsh media criticism. The special election to fill the vacancy left by the resignation of speaker-elect Bob Livingston is a good example of how this can happen.[28] In Louisiana's open election system all candidates from all parties compete head-to-head in the primary contest. If no candidate receives a majority of the vote, the top two candidates compete in a runoff election. David Treen, the first Republican to be elected governor since Reconstruction, emerged as the front-runner and GOP favorite. He was pitted against former state legislator and Ku Klux Klan grand wizard David Duke, ophthalmologist Monica Monica, and state legislator David Vitter. Monica polled second early in the race because of her unusual name, her pledge to put $500,000 of her own money into her campaign, and her early television ads. Her first round of ads presented her as a citizen legislator in contrast to the politicians competing for the seat. Monica also benefited from issue advocacy ads financed by Americans for Limited Terms (ALT) after signing a pledge to limit herself to three terms in Congress.

The ad run by ALT marked the beginning of Monica's demise. The ad included footage from Monica's own ads suggesting improper coordination with Monica's campaign, and attacked Vitter, a champion of term limits at the legislative level, for not taking a three-term pledge for Congress. Vitter responded with an ad that began, "Monica Monica and her out-of-state allies are lying about David Vitter."[29] Monica retorted with an ad of her own that said the following:

> David Vitter—he's so bitter. When a political opponent asked if he authored the gay rights bill, he became angry, agitated. His reaction was so outrageous he was sued for assault and battery by the woman, and found liable by the court. Now, Vitter has attacked yet another woman—Dr. Monica Monica....[30]

Afterward, Monica ran an attack against Treen stating that a New Orleans casino had paid him thousands of dollars for lobbying services and that Treen had failed to register with the state as a lobbyist.[31] Treen rebuffed the ad with a television advertisement that reinforced the message of Vitter's earlier reply to Monica:

> In the last few days, thousands of negative phone calls and TV ads have been spreading lies about me and other candidates.... Monica Monica and her out-of-state backers are trying to destroy my reputation. This is the kind of dirty Louisiana politics I've fought against my entire life.[32]

Monica's attack ads, and the controversy over improper coordination with the ALT's issue advocacy campaign, eroded her "citizen legislator" image. A local political strategist observed, "In two weeks after she got involved in attacks and counters, her favorable ratings collapsed from a five-to-one positive-to-negative ratio to a nearly one-to-one ratio, which was disaster for her."[33] Monica fell from her early position of a close second to finish fourth in the primary.

Though these examples show that negative advertising occasionally can be boon or bust for a candidate, generally speaking, negative ads do little to boost a candidate's electoral performance. Our findings shore up the observation of Ray Strother, president of the American Association of Political Consultants, that "the combative mode does not work anymore" because negative ads have reached their saturation point.[34] Voters appear to distrust negative information, find negative ads unconvincing, or believe that most negative allegations are irrelevant to governing.

Even in cases where negative advertising appears to influence election outcomes, it is a mistake to attribute too much weight to negative ads. For example, Democrat David Wu won a hard-fought open-seat race in Oregon's 1st district with 52 percent of the vote. In early October Wu attacked his opponent, Republican Molly Bordonaro, with television ads that accused Bordonaro of wanting to raise the eligibility age for Social Security and cut benefits in the program. In the final week before the election, Wu ran ads that portrayed Bordonaro as flip-flopping on issues. This ad used excerpts from an interview taped during Bordonaro's 1996 congressional campaign in which she said she would be a "spokesperson for vouchers" in Congress and would work to eliminate the U.S. Department of Education. Bordonaro had dropped both of these positions in her 1998 campaign. The ads put Bordonaro on the defensive during the critical final week of campaigning.

Though some commentators described the school-vouchers attack ad as the turning point of the campaign, the outcome was probably not decided by these negative ads. Wu's strengths were considerable. Wu had gained electoral experience working on presidential campaigns for both Gary Hart and Walter Mondale, and ran an exceptionally professional campaign, which was staffed by many nationally renowned consultants. Wu hired the Campaign Performance Group and Terris and Jaye for direct mail; the Global Strategy Group, Hamilton and Staff, and Ridder Braden for polling; and Murphy Putnam Media and Nordlinger Associates for media services. These strengths, combined with Bordonaro's weaknesses, led to Wu's victory. Bordonaro's name recognition, campaign organization, and fund-raising network from the previous election allowed her to gain an initial lead against Wu. However, her lead faltered because she did not develop a persuasive campaign message. She failed to identify any compelling wedge issues to distinguish herself from Wu, relying instead on valence issues like increasing funding for law enforcement.[35]

Candidate status, district partisanship, and campaign spending also have significant effects on election outcomes. Challengers typically receive about 13 percent fewer points than incumbents; open-seat contestants receive about 3.5 percent less. For every 10 percent of the electorate that shares a candidate's party identification, the candidate receives another 2 percent of the vote. Political experience helps candidates. Candidates who have previously held elective office win about 3 percent more of the vote than do unelected politicians—candidates who have served as legislative or executive branch aides, political appointees, state, local, or national party officials, or political consultants, or have previously waged an unsuccessful bid for Congress. Unelected politicians, in turn, win about 3 percent more of the vote than do political amateurs. Finally, candidates who receive more media coverage than their opponent or receive endorsements by local media over their opponent typically receive approximately 4 percent more of the vote.

CONCLUSION

Most candidates for the House of Representatives run highly professional and fairly negative campaigns, and the professionalism of these campaigns is at least partly responsible for their negative tone. Many campaign professionals believe that negative ads win elections, and their beliefs are reflected in the conduct of the campaigns that employ them. Candidates have good reason to trust the advice of their consultants and professional staffs. Professional campaigns consistently outperform amateur campaigns, and most candidates are wont to take advice from the experienced political aides and consultants whose services they contract at a considerable premium. Nevertheless, political professionals are mistaken in their confidence that negative advertising wins elections. Although negative ads may occasionally undermine an opponent's support, they can also backfire and drag down the candidate who pays for them. The evidence shows that negative ads do not strengthen a House candidate's performance at the polls. Candidates who run positive campaigns can get elected to Congress.

Our research reinforces the work of others who have observed that campaigns in competitive races are very negative. The rise of campaign advertising by political parties and interest groups, which tends to be more negative in tone than candidate ads, have accentuated this trend. Because voters have a hard time differentiating the candidate ads from the party and interest group ads, it is often the candidates who are blamed by voters for the increasingly negative tone of American electoral politics.

Whether our assessment that candidates who run positive campaigns can get elected to Congress will remain true if there is a general shift towards more positive ads is difficult to know. It is, however, a hopeful note that in an era known for hardball politics and negative advertising, campaigns that go negative no longer reap an electoral dividend.

APPENDIX A: THE 1998 CONGRESSIONAL CAMPAIGN STUDY

The 1998 Congressional Campaign Study consisted of a survey of all congressional campaigns competing in major-party contested House elections. A letter was sent two weeks before election day to the campaign headquarters of all major-party general election candidates describing the project and requesting an appointment to conduct a telephone interview. The letter included a copy of the survey instrument and invited the respondents to submit their completed questionnaire by fax or mail, instead of answering questions in a telephone interview. Twenty-three percent exercised the fax/mail option. The remaining 77 percent participated in telephone interviews that were conducted between November 4 and November 13. The response rate for the entire survey was 44 percent, and the sample represents the underlying population of candidates on important characteristics such as party, status, and electoral success (see Table A-1).

TABLE A-1   REPRESENTATIVENESS OF THE 1998 CONGRESSIONAL SURVEY (%)

	SURVEY RESPONDENTS	ALL CANDIDATES
Candidate Status		
Incumbents	46	52
Challengers	45	39
Open seats	9	9
Electoral Success		
Winners	47	44
Losers	52	56
Party Affiliation		
Democrats	45	49
Republicans	55	51
(N)	(336)	(771)

APPENDIX B: OPERATIONALIZATION OF THE VARIABLES

Campaign professionalism is measured using an index calculated by summing the number of campaign activities performed by campaign professionals, defined as either independent political consultants or paid campaign aides. Campaigns that reported hiring professionals to perform campaign management, media advertising, press relations, issue and opposition research, polling, fund-raising, get-out-the-vote activities, legal advice, and accounting/filing FEC reports received a score of 9. Campaigns that reported hiring campaign professionals for none of these positions received the lowest score of 0.

Candidate status is measured using two dummy variables. The variable *challenger* is coded 1 if the candidate was a challenger in the general election. The variable *open seat* is coded 1 if the candidate was running for an open seat. Incumbents were coded 0 for both variables.

Partisan bias of the district is measured by subtracting the percentage of voters who identified with the candidate's party minus the percentage who identified with the opponent's party.

Negative advertising is measured using the respondents' answers to the following question: "Did your campaign or your opponent's campaign use negative advertising?" Self-reported assessments of negativity may not be as accurate as a measure of negativity produced using a content analysis of campaign advertising, but this measure is reliable. Competitors in the same race mostly agreed on the negativity of their own and each other's campaigns. In districts where both campaigns responded to the survey, 43 percent agreed on their evaluations of both campaigns, and only 3 percent gave opposing evaluations of both campaigns. In the remaining districts, campaigns were in partial agreement. In these cases, most campaigns underevaluated the negativity of their own campaign or overevaluated their opponent's negativity. The result is a somewhat conservative measure of negativity. The variable *campaign used negative ads* is coded 1 if the respondent indicated that their campaign or both campaigns used negative advertising, and 0 otherwise. The variable *opponent used negative ads* is created by matching candidates with their opponents' survey responses.

Electoral competitiveness is measured using a 3-point scale modified from the *Cook Political Report*'s rating of House race competitiveness. Safe seats are coded 0, competitive seats that are leaning toward one party are coded 1, and tossups are coded as 3.

Political experience is coded 0 for political amateurs, 1 for unelected politicians (those who have been legislative or executive branch aides, political appointees, state or local party officials, or political consultants, or have previously run an unsuccessful campaign for Congress), and 2 for candidates who have previously held elective office.

Media advantage is coded 1 if the campaign reported that their candidate received more news coverage than the opponent or if the campaign reported that their candidate received an endorsement from the local media but their opponent did not receive an endorsement.

The campaign communications spending and independent expenditures variables are derived from the 1998 Congressional Campaign Study and the FEC's 1998 candidate summary file. The measure of *campaign communications spending* was calculated by multiplying the proportion of campaign expenditures that respondents to the survey budgeted for communications and the total expenditures reported by the FEC (minus contributions given to other candidates). In cases where a candidate's opponent did not participate in the survey, campaign communications are estimated using the average proportion of expenditures used by survey respondents who had the same incumbency status and were involved in elections of a similar level of competitiveness. *Independent expenditures* are the sum of independent expenditures for the candidate or against the candidate made by PACs and parties.

ACKNOWLEDGMENT

The research for this chapter was sponsored by a grant from The Pew Charitable Trusts. The opinions expressed in this chapter are those of the authors and do not necessarily reflect the views of The Pew Charitable Trusts.

NOTES

1. Robert G. Meadow, ed., *New Communication Technologies in Politics* (Washington, DC: The Washington Program of the Annenberg School of Communications, 1985), 8–9; Richard K. Scher, *The Modern Political Campaign*. (Armonk, NY: M. E. Sharpe, 1997), 27–48.
2. Robert Agranoff, "The New Style of Campaigning: The Decline of Party and the Rise of Candidate Centered Technology," in Robert Agranoff, ed., *The New Style in Election Campaigns* (Boston: Holbrook Press, 1972), 3–50; Paul S. Herrnson, *Congressional Elections: Campaigning at Home and in Washington*, 3rd ed. (Washington, DC: CQ Press, 2000), ch. 3; Meadow, *New Communication Technologies*.
3. Agranoff, "The New Style of Campaigning"; Dan Nimmo, *The Political Persuaders* (Englewood Cliffs, NJ: Prentice-Hall, 1970), 34–38.
4. Paul Herrnson, Kelly Patterson, and John Pitney, "From Ward Heelers to Public Relations Experts: The Parties to Respond to Mass Politics," in Stephen C. Craig, ed., *Broken Contract? Changing Relationships between Citizens and Government in the United States* (Boulder, CO: Westview Press, 1996), 251–267; Mark P. Petracca, "Political Consultants and Democratic Governance," *PS: Political Science and Politics* 22 (1989): 11–14.
5. Larry J. Sabato, *The Rise of Political Consultants: New Ways of Winning Elections* (New York: Basic Books, 1981), 165–166; Barbara G. Salmore and Stephen A. Salmore,

Candidates, Parties and Campaigns: Electoral Politics in America, 2nd ed. (Washington, DC: CQ Press, 1989), 159.

6. The Pew Research Center, "The View of Political Consultants: Don't Blame Us," June 17, 1998.

7. Agranoff, *The New Style in Election Campaigns*, 52–58; Sabato, *The Rise of Political Consultants*, 8–10; James A. Thurber and Candice J. Nelson, eds., *Campaigns and Elections American Style* (Boulder, CO: Westview Press, 1995), 2–5.

8. Jay Bryant, "Paid Media Advertising," in Thurber and Nelson, *Campaigns and Elections American Style*, 87–99.

9. Herrnson, *Congressional Elections*, ch. 3.

10. Ibid., 235.

11. Similarly, 51 percent of all ads run by House candidates in the top 75 media markets were positive. See Goldstein et al., "Going Negative: Attack Advertising in the 1998 Elections," Chapter 5 in this volume.

12. Self-reported use of negative advertising is calculated by adding candidate only and both candidate and opponent rows in Table 4-2.

13. "Inside Politics," *Campaigns & Elections*, December 1998/January 1999, 9.

14. David Gibson, "Bishops to Pressure Pro-Choice Candidates," *The Record*, November 13, 1998, A3.

15. "Media Mix," *Campaigns & Elections*, August 1999, 71.

16. Probabilities are conditional effects probabilities calculated while holding all other variables at their mean value. See Scott Menard, *Applied Logistic Regression Analysis* (Thousand Oaks, CA: Sage Publications, 1995), 43–44.

17. Robert Schlesinger, "Candidates Run Impeachment Ads," *The Hill*, October 21, 1998, 3.

18. Bryant, "Paid Media Advertising," 97–99.

19. Philip D. Duncan and Christine C. Lawrence, eds., *Congressional Quarterly's Politics in America: 1998, The 105th Congress* (Washington, DC: CQ Press, 1997), 692.

20. John Laidler, "Tierney, Torkildsen Revive Duel in 6th District Election," *Boston Globe*, October 4, 1998, Northwest Weekly, 6; John Laidler and Anthony Flint, "McGovern, Tierney, Delahunt Win," *Boston Globe*, November 4, 1998, Metro/Region, B9.

21. See David B. Magleby, "The Expanded Role of Interest Groups and Political Parties in Competitive U.S. Congressional Elections," in David B. Magleby, ed., *Outside Money, Soft Money, and Issue Advocacy in the 1998 Congressional Elections* (Lanham, MD: Rowlan and Littlefield, 2000), 45.

22. Philip Dacey, "Mighty Casey Struck Out: Analysis of the 1998 Congressional Election in Pennsylvania District 10," December 9, 1998, unpublished paper.

23. "Whoops!," *National Journal's House Race Hotline*, November 2, 1998, Section: Freshmen.

24. See case studies in Michael A. Bailey, Ronald A. Faucheux, Paul S. Herrnson, and Clyde Wilcox, eds., *Campaigns and Elections: Contemporary Case Studies* (Washington, DC: CQ Press, 1999).

25. David Beiler, "Twinkle, Twinkle Kenneth Starr: How Physicist Rush Holt Used the Clinton Scandal to Oust a Republican Congressman," *Campaigns & Elections*, May 1999, 46.

26. Ibid., 49.

27. David T. Canon and Paul S. Herrnson, "First Things First: Democrat Tammy Baldwin's Wisconsin Win Blended Professionalism, People Power," *Campaigns & Elections*, May 1999, 50–54.

28. Kristin Brainerd, "Three Davids, No Goliath and Plenty of Slingshots: How Reformer David Vitter Won the Special Election to Fill Bob Livingston's Vacant Louisiana House Seat," *Campaigns & Elections*, September 1999, 35–47.

29. Ibid., 39.

30. "Treen Holds Slight Lead," *The Bulletin's Front Runner*, April 30, 1999.

31. Steve Ritea, "Record Amount Spent in Race; 1st District Election Costliest in History," *Times-Picayune*, August 13, 1999, A1.

32. "Treen Holds Slight Lead."

33. Brainerd, "Three Davids, No Goliath," 42.

34. Quoted in Bard Rourke, "Taking the Pledge: Codes of Conduct," *Campaigns & Elections*, August 1999, 69.

35. For an analysis of this campaign, see Russ Dondero, "Oregon First District," in David B. Magleby and Marianne Holt, eds., *Outside Money: Soft Money & Issue Ads in Competitive 1998 Congressional Elections: A Report of a Grant Funded by the Pew Charitable Trusts* (Washington, DC: February 1999), 155–164.

5

GOING NEGATIVE: ATTACK
ADVERTISING IN THE 1998 ELECTIONS

KENNETH M. GOLDSTEIN | JONATHAN S. KRASNO

LEE BRADFORD | DANIEL E. SELTZ

Much of the money that candidates for Congress take so much time to raise is spent on television advertising. In many House races and in most Senate races, television advertising is the single largest expenditure in the campaign and is the chief way that candidates for Congress communicate their messages to voters. Moreover, television advertising is the preferred way for parties and interest groups to take advantage of loopholes in current election law and to channel resources in support of their favored candidates. To put it briefly, television commercials are one of the most important tools in the arsenal of a modern congressional campaign.

Not surprisingly, the candidates who raise all this money for television advertising and the consultants who spend it believe that TV ads matter. Scholars are not so sure: There has been considerable debate on the effect and effectiveness of the television air war in congressional campaigns. In fact, for decades, the conventional wisdom among academics has tended to downplay the influence of paid advertising and even the impact of campaign spending by the heaviest spenders—incumbents—on election outcomes.[1] More recent studies, however, indicate that campaign spending in general, and advertising in particular, has a relatively small—but politically significant—influence on individual voters and on election outcome.[2] While fundamental factors such as incumbency, the quality of candidates, and the partisan composition of a congressional district explain most of the variation in election outcomes, advertising may play an important role at the margin in determining who wins and who loses.

Political consultants, of course, do not earn their often hefty fees by simply telling candidates to spend money or to advertise on television if they can afford it. Campaigns offer scores of strategic decisions, among them the question of what sort of television commercials to run. Of particular interest here to all observers—citizens, journalists, and academics—are so-called attack ads, the short spots that attempt to expose some of the failings, real or fabricated, of the opposing candidate. Citizens, journalists, and even some scholars decry negative campaigning, arguing among other things that it depresses turnout. Other scholars claim that such advertising may actually mobilize voters.[3]

Political consultants, less concerned about the health of the body politic than about winning, swear by negative tactics.[4] The beliefs of ad makers appear to be backed up by at least some social science theory. For example, scholars have asserted that negative information tends to be more salient, and therefore is more influential than positive information.[5] Still, there is little empirical evidence from congressional elections to support claims that negative campaigns are more effective.[6] Whatever one's position on the effect of attack advertising, better empirical research and an improved understanding of how attack advertising is used are clearly needed.

Despite the heated rhetoric about the ubiquity of negative campaigning, not every race automatically descends to the supposed gutter of attack and counterattack. The decision to attack depends on a variety of strategic considerations. In this chapter, we explore a few of these considerations, making use of a remarkable new data set to examine television advertising in the 1998 congressional elections. We begin by describing a new satellite tracking system that allows us to look at campaign advertising in a significantly greater level of detail than previous work. We explain how the data were coded and discuss the different advertisers who sponsored political commercials in 1998. We then focus our analysis on two different questions about the use of attack ads in the 1998 elections: Who uses attack ads? and Where are these ads most likely to appear?

The CMAG Data

In the past, the only way to get information on the frequency and targeting of television advertising was to attempt to obtain information from usually uncooperative and unreliable campaign organizations, or to go through the arduous process of calling individual stations in selected markets and examining their advertising logs. In either case, serious questions about the accuracy of the data would remain.

Fortunately, an independent satellite tracking system developed by Competitive Media Reporting (CMR) and marketed in the political field by Campaign Media Analysis Group (CMAG) now automatically monitors political advertising activity throughout the year. The CMAG system tracks the satellite transmissions of the national networks (ABC, CBS, NBC, and Fox) as well as 25 national cable networks (CNN, ESPN, TNT, and so on). More important, the ad detector system monitors advertising in each of the nation's top 75 media markets. The system's software recognizes the electronic seams between programming and advertising, and identifies the "digital fingerprints" of specific advertisements. When the system does not recognize the fingerprint of a particular commercial spot, the storyboard (the full audio and one frame every four seconds of video) is captured and downloaded to the firm's headquarters. Analysts then tag the ad with a unique digital code. Thereafter, the system automatically recognizes and logs that particular commercial wherever and whenever it airs. This technology was originally developed by the U.S. Navy to track Soviet submarines during the cold war. Its original commercial application was for large corporations to track competitors' advertisements and to confirm that their own advertisements were being aired.

The quantity and quality of the CMAG data are remarkable. The database contains information on the content, timing, and geographic targeting of every campaign commercial broadcast, regardless of its sponsor. Although campaign finance laws may allow differential levels of reporting by candidates, parties, and interest groups depending on their ability to disguise their appeals as issue advocacy, the CMAG system recognizes no such niceties, logging every political commercial regardless of sponsor and legal category.[7] As a result, a major strength of the CMAG database is that it contains information on spots aired by the candidates *and* information about the spots aired by their allies. The latter turns out to be particularly important when we examine negative advertising. The data set includes the specific media market where the ad was aired, who aired it, the date and time of each individual airing, the program on which the ad was aired, as well as the cost and ratings points per airing. By treating each time an ad was broadcast as the unit of analysis in this chapter, we were able to give appropriate weight to the frequency in which a commercial was shown.

CMAG provided us with information on every political advertisement that was aired in a top 75 market in the 1998 elections. This included almost 2,000 different spots on behalf of House and Senate candidates that aired nearly 300,000 times. The top 75 markets reached about 80 percent of households in the United States, but the resulting data set contains commercials from fewer than 80 percent of the House and Senate races in 1998. Instead "just" 190 races are covered—160 House contests and 30 Senate contests. The reason is simple: Many House candidates did not bother to broadcast television commercials. That is particularly true of House candidates in the largest, most expensive media markets.[8] The resulting data set, nevertheless, is the most comprehensive source of information about political campaigns and contains 50 races where the candidates, parties, and interest groups combined to broadcast more than 1,000 ads.

From our perspective, one of the greatest strengths of the CMAG data is that they provide information about the content of the ads. One of the key features of the system is that it generates a "storyboard"—a frame of video every four seconds and full text of the audio—for every advertisement. We used these storyboards to analyze extensively the content (tone, language, issues mentioned, and style) of each of the ads, designing a questionnaire for use by half a dozen coders as they examined the commercials.[9]

Of all advertisements aired, 49 percent promoted candidates, while just 27 percent were attack ads. Twenty percent were spots that contrasted the positions of the two candidates. The tone of the remaining 4 percent of the ads was unclear. The answer to the question of whether the proportion of ads that were attack ads is surprisingly high or low depends, of course, on one's perspective. The quarter of ads that attacked other candidates may seem somewhat anticlimactic in the face of some of the more expansive complaints about contenders' willingness to savage one another. But our judgment of how negative the campaigns in 1998 really were also depends on how we regard the 20 percent of commercials that coders rated as contrast ads. A quick perusal of the storyboards that fell in this category suggests that most of these ads tended to focus more on the deficiencies of the opposing candidate than on the virtues of the favorite, making many of them a somewhat toned-down version of a "pure" attack ad (see Figure 5-1 on page 96). Nevertheless, the difference between the two types of ads is obvious, for one mentions the favored candidate, while the other does not. If peeved viewers want to know whom to blame for negative attacks carried too far, contrast ads make it very clear.

Nor, of course, is every attack (or contrast) ad equally vicious. The type of commercial that has received the most complaints in the press—the ones focusing on the personal characteristics of the candidates—turns out to be relatively rare. Two in 3 ads aired in 1998 dealt solely with policy issues, and only a little over 1 in 10 (11 percent) focused on candidates' personal qualities. The remaining dealt with both personal and policy issues. Furthermore, the ads that emphasized personal issues were much more likely to be positive—such as biographical spots about a candidate or introductions to her family—than attack ads.

Incumbents, challengers, and candidates for open seats differ in their propensities to use negative ads. The same is true of candidates and parties, as well as candidates who are in different types of districts. Using these systematic data in conjunction with illustrative examples from particular races, we give a nuanced analysis of the nature of campaign advertising in general and of attack advertising in particular in 1998 contests.

WHO GOES NEGATIVE?

Naturally, not every advertiser is equally willing or, more likely, finds it necessary to attack the opposing side. The most obvious exception, at least in theory, to the assumptions about the popularity of negative campaigning is

FIGURE 5-1   POSITIVE ADS, ATTACK ADS, AND CONTRAST ADS

POSITIVE AD / EDWARDS FOR SENATE

EDWARDS: When I was growing up here in Robins people knew right from wrong. They knew they had to take responsibility for their actions. We have to get back to that way of thinking.

ANNOUNCER: John Edwards, endorsed for the Senate by North Carolina's police.

EDWARDS: I support the death penalty, 100,000 new police on the streets, an end to foreign aid for countries that export drugs to the United States. And to protect our kids, we should prohibit anyone with a criminal record from working in a daycare center.

ANNOUNCER: John Edwards, the people's Senator.

ATTACK AD / D'AMATO FOR SENATE

ANNOUNCER: This year alone, Chuck Schumer missed over one hundred votes in Congress, the worst attendance record of the thirty-one New York Congressmen. He missed the vote to hire 100,000 new teachers. He missed the vote to save Social Security, the vote to improve breast cancer screening. He even missed the vote on healthcare for veterans. Chuck Schumer—always putting politics over people. Chuck Schumer—full-time pay, part-time work.

CONTRAST AD / CHAIREZ FOR CONGRESS

ANNOUNCER: Judge Don Chairez took an oath to do what's right.

CHAIREZ: My opponent is misleading you. As a judge in the Stromeyer case I kept in the critical confession which caused the defendant to plead guilty. That's why he'll be in prison the rest of his life.

ANNOUNCER: Named Law Enforcement Judge of the Year, Chairez has spent a career being tough on crime. Shelley Berkley has spent her career supporting backroom deals actually advising her boss to try to buy off judges. So you decide. A politician who wants to buy off judges or a judge who can't be bought. Don Chairez for Congress.

---

incumbents. Far from being poster boys for campaign manners, incumbents' assumed preference for promotional spots stems from a basic political calculation. Incumbents, after all, have records of accomplishment to publicize in their quest to hold on to their jobs. Challengers undoubtedly have accomplishments, too, but likely none are quite so relevant to the job of senator or representative as the incumbent's performance in that very office. Thus, the textbook campaign has incumbents reminding voters of all of the good things that they have achieved in office, as challengers struggle to break the inertia of reelection by criticizing the incumbents' performance.[10]

Twenty years ago many candidates and consultants believed that incumbents were in such a favorable position that they should not acknowledge their opponents in any way, so as to avoid giving the challengers free publicity. Few incumbents would take the same position today, yet most accounts would still have incumbents engaging in less attack advertising than their opponents. This expectation is borne out in our examination of the CMAG data: 65 percent of incumbents' ads were positive and only 17 percent were pure attack ads. For challengers, however, the opposite was true: 42 percent of challengers' ads were pure attack ads, while just 36 percent of challengers' ads were aimed exclusively at promoting their candidacies.

In North Carolina's 4th district, for example, Representative David Price faced a spirited challenge from Republican Tom Rohberg. All of Price's ads were rated by coders as promotional, though Rohberg was on the receiving end of a blast of attack ads sponsored by the AFL-CIO. By comparison, none of Rohberg's ads focused mainly on promoting his candidacy. Instead, 4 in 10 of his commercials were attack ads, with the remainder contrasting him with Price. Somewhat surprisingly (as we will see below), it was the Republican Party that sponsored ads promoting Rohberg in October, after a big wave of attack advertising by his campaign in September.

The race in North Carolina's 4th district serves as a reminder of the most important change in congressional elections in the last half dozen years. Thanks to the advent of issue advocacy, parties and interest groups are now able to circumvent campaign finance laws to engage in virtually unlimited electioneering in House and Senate races. This development stems from courts' refusal to consider messages that do not contain the so-called "magic words of express advocacy" such as "vote for," "vote against," "support," or "defeat" as campaigning.[11] The result has allowed parties and interest groups to use money raised without the limitations that affect candidates and to spend this money, without reporting it, on advertising that is virtually indistinguishable from candidate ads.[12]

Political parties were particularly big players in 1998's congressional campaigns. The CMAG data show that parties ran 44,998 ads in the top 75 media markets, compared with 22,249 by interest groups, though over half of interest-group ads were rated by coders as focused on issues, not candidates. Parties and groups were both outstripped by candidates (235,791 ads), though not always. The data show just two races where more than 1,000 ads were aired and where candidates purchased less than half the advertising, but many others where parties (and more occasionally groups) were substantial presences. The sheer amount of advertising by parties makes it necessary to examine the tone of their ads.

The comparison in the tone of candidate ads and party ads was stark. Fifty-six percent of commercials sponsored by candidates focused on promoting their virtues, with less than 21 percent attacking their opponent. For parties, on the other hand, these proportions were practically reversed: 6 in 10 attacked candidates, while 28 percent promoted candidates. This division of labor is quite curious. Why, aside from a few exceptions like Tom Rohberg, would candidates rely on parties to soften up their opponents? The answer, most likely, involves another piece of conventional wisdom about negative campaigning: the notion that attack ads damage the image of those who broadcast them. Put another (familiar) way, in a mud fight everyone gets dirty. In the end, candidates generally would rather not be seen as too mean.[13]

For candidates, then, this arrangement is quite convenient. Parties are left with the task of softening up the opposition, while the candidates can pretend to float above the fray. How convincing candidates' claims of innocence are is quite debatable. It is hard to imagine that voters discern much distinction between campaign ads sponsored by candidates and ads sponsored by their parties, especially when the two sets of ads use many of the same visuals and emphasize the same themes. Nevertheless, in race after race, the most vicious attacks came from political parties, not from the candidates.[14]

Of course, there are exceptions. New York's Senate race—by far 1998's most expensive contest—featured two heavyweight contenders, incumbent senator Al D'Amato and Democratic representative Charles Schumer, both known for their hard-hitting styles and their fund-raising ability. Given their reputations, neither candidate had much to lose from attacking the other, and both did so with gusto. Less than 4 in 10 spots in both campaigns were promotional, and D'Amato, in particular, ran a sizable number of attack ads. The parties chimed in, of course, with even more lopsidedly negative campaigns of their own, but the candidates carried most of the burden.

One of the interesting things about this situation is what it means for political parties. Parties, of course, are a particular concern of political scientists, who have long argued for strengthening these vital institutions.[15] As a result, many scholars have applauded the new fiscal muscle that political parties have acquired in the last decades, viewing it as a sign of renewed vigor. In fact, the law that allows political parties to solicit growing amounts of soft money—money raised outside contribution and spending limits—is supposedly for the purposes of allowing the parties to strengthen their organizations, carry out grass-roots campaign efforts, and perform other "party-building" activities.[16] Our data show, however, that little of the advertising that parties do could be viewed as building up the strength of the party.

Examples abound. In Wisconsin, for instance, the state GOP ran a commercial praising its senatorial nominee, Representative Mark Neumann, for "standing up against his own party" in fights over Social Security. But as outrageous as this and some of the other commercials we examined are, the most telling facts are these statistics: Just 15 percent of party ads mentioned either political party by name, but 99 percent of these ads mentioned a political candidate. There seems little doubt, in light of these patterns, that the advertising that political parties do is intended first and foremost to aid their candidates, not enhance in any way their public standing.

STRATEGIC CONSIDERATIONS

In most congressional campaigns, there is little doubt about the eventual outcome. The overwhelming majority of incumbents win reelection, and even most open seats have characteristics that strongly predispose them toward one party or another. In fact, two weeks before Election Day in 1998, pre-election handicapper Charlie Cook ranked only 62 out of the 435 House races at stake as competitive.[17] Furthermore, he ranked only 26 contests as complete tossups that could go either way. On a proportional basis, matters were more competitive on the Senate side, where 11 out of 34 seats were in doubt in the weeks leading up to the election, with 4 being complete tossups. Although Democratic congressional candidates ended up doing better than all the pundits had predicted, when all was said and done, only 41 House races were decided by less than 10 percentage points—a commonly used measure of whether or not a race was competitive—and only six incumbents lost their bids for reelection.

The question is whether the competitiveness of a race had a significant influence on the tone of the advertising. A quick look at a few specific races suggests that it did. For example, the race in the 1st district in Nevada was one of the most competitive in the country as well as being one of the most negative. In that contest, Democrat Shelley Berkley should have been a prohibitive favorite in a district where Democrats outnumber Republicans by nearly 42,000 registered voters. However, in early June of 1998, the Berkley campaign was rocked by a tape recording in which she was heard telling her former boss, Las Vegas Sands, Inc., chairman Sheldon Adelson, to use his power and money to influence local politicians. The polls immediately tightened, and the national party committees focused on this newly competitive race. Republican candidate Don Chairez, the Republican Party, and their interest-group allies spent over $800,000 dollars airing over 1,000 spots—most of which targeted Berkley's ethical problems. The tag line used over and over again was "Fairness not favors."[18]

Chairez, on the other hand, had his own problems, which became ammunition for attack ads targeted at him. First, Berkley and her allies hit Chairez for a series of rulings he had made from the bench. Second, Chairez had been hit with liens for not paying taxes more than a decade ago.[19] Third, Chairez faced embarrassing headlines as a result of a sex discrimination complaint filed by a former secretary, who accused him of creating a hostile work environment and then firing her when she complained.[20] After all was said and aired in this race where over 60 percent of the ads contained some form of an attack, Berkley won by less than 3 percentage points.

The race between Baron Hill and Jean Leising in Indiana's 9th Distinct was just as close and even more negative. Hill, the Democrat, and Leising, the Republican, were competing to replace long-time incumbent Lee Hamilton in a district where the vote for the major candidates in the last two presidential elections had been virtually even. All in all, 8 in 10 ads aired in the race had some sort of an attack on the opponent, with 67 percent being pure attack ads. Two attack ads, in particular, garnered much attention and were credited by consultants as helping put Hill over the top. In one, Hill said that Leising wanted to abolish federal education funding, and in the second he said she wanted to privatize Social Security.[21]

Kentucky was home to one of the most competitive and negative Senate races in the country. In this open-seat contest, former major league baseball pitcher Jim Bunning, the Republican candidate, faced former University of Kentucky basketball player Scotty Baesler. Both candidates spent over $1 million on television advertising, with their respective parties throwing in an additional $500,000. All in all, over 12,000 individual spots were aired and 65 percent attacked the opponent in some way. However, in a pattern similar to the one described in the preceding section, Baesler and Bunning both refrained from running many negative advertisements, letting their respective parties do the dirty work. Nearly 8 in 10 advertisements aired by the Democratic Party were negative, while about 6 in 10 advertisements run by the Republican Party were negative. In one of the most prominent ads of the whole electoral cycle, the Republicans aired a spot with Wagner's "Ride of the Valkyries" playing in the background that made Baesler look like Hitler delivering a speech. In another well-known spot, Bunning ran an ad showing actors thanking Baesler, in Spanish and (with subtitles) Chinese, for voting for the North American Free Trade Agreement (NAFTA) and Most Favored Nation (MFN) status for China.[22] Bunning ended up besting Baesler by a few thousand votes in the closest Senate race in 1998.

A significantly less competitive race for the Senate occurred in Florida. Bob Graham, the Democratic incumbent, had won four straight statewide elections, dating back to 1978 when he became governor, and polls indicated that he was ahead by a comfortable 30 percent point margin for most of the race. His opponent, Charlie Crist, spent nearly two years campaigning against Graham, but in the end was outspent by a 4 to 1 margin and garnered only 38 percent of the vote. In this lopsided race, 83 percent of the ads aired by the candidates were positive, and there were no pure attack ads run.

There were even more races on the House side that were similarly uncompetitive and similarly positive in tone. In the contest between Democratic incumbent Louise Slaughter and Republican challenger Richard Kaplan in New York's 28th congressional district, Slaughter beat Kaplan by over a 2 to 1 margin and not a single attack advertisement was aired. Kaplan put more on the air than Slaughter, but all the spots were promoting his social and economic plans. Although outspent on the air, Slaughter never felt threatened, and responded with positive spots about her record on women's issues and fighting for the district.

Given this series of examples, can we generalize from these few cases that candidates and their allies in competitive contests are more likely to use attack advertising? The answer is yes. Among ads aired in the 160 House races in our data, almost half contained at least a partial attack (see Figure 5-2). Fifty-three percent of the ads aired by all House candidates were positive.

Candidates in closely contested House election contests were more likely to go negative than were others. In competitive races, 54 percent of the spots aired attacked the opponent, whereas in uncompetitive races, 39 percent attacked an opposing candidate. Similarly, 62 percent of the ads aired in competitive Senate races had at least some attack messages, while only 26 percent of the spots in noncompetitive races attacked one of the candidates (see Figure 5-3 on page 102).

The heavy use of attack ads in competitive races sheds some light on our earlier discussion of negative campaigning by incumbents and challengers. Obviously, a race that is competitive for an incumbent is also competitive for a challenger, but because of their superior fund-raising ability, the incumbents ran 50 percent more ads than did their opponents. The incumbents' advantage is especially pronounced in less competitive races, where they ran 154 percent more ads. The reason is fairly simple: Incumbents in noncompetitive races still have the ability to raise and spend substantial amounts of money, while challengers do not. Challengers who ran ads were competing disproportionately in the tightest races.

FIGURE 5-2   TONES OF ADS IN HOUSE RACES

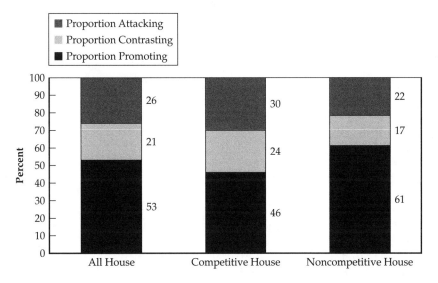

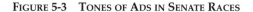

FIGURE 5-3   TONES OF ADS IN SENATE RACES

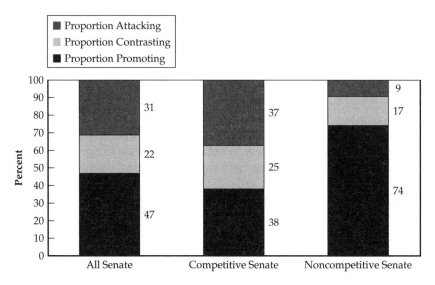

The propensity of challengers to attack is even more understandable in these circumstances. It is not enough for these nonincumbents merely to present the case for themselves; they must also somehow convince voters to make a change. Creating doubt about the incumbent is the first step in making voters want to make a change. Still, some scholars have argued that challengers are unlikely to wage a negative campaign when they have little chance of winning because they are wary about hurting their own reputation and damaging their own professional or political futures.[23] This discrepancy can be explained by looking a little more carefully at the type of challengers who aired any advertising at all. More than one-third of challengers in the CMAG data set did not air any advertising whatsoever. These were the candidates who were in the least competitive races. Challengers in many of the other races were somewhat more competitive and decided to air a significant proportion of attack spots.

In the preceding section we discussed how parties are much more likely to go on the attack. Looking at the data by the competitiveness of the race illustrates the not-so-surprising fact that the parties act strategically and tend to get involved in the more competitive contests. The CMAG data reveal that 92 percent of the party spots aired in Senate races were aired in competitive races. The CMAG data also reveal that 60 percent of the party spots aired in House races were aired in competitive races. Still, even holding the competitiveness of the races constant, we see that parties were more likely to go negative. For example, in competitive races, 43 percent of candidate ads aired had some sort of attack, while 68 percent of party ads had some sort of attack. In some cases, such as the Kentucky Senate race, there was clearly some sort of division of labor between the sponsors of various ads, with candidates promoting themselves and party and interest groups tearing down the opposition.

These facts have profound implications for the effects of attack advertising on both election outcome and voter participation. If parties and interest groups focus most of their attack advertising in competitive elections and these elections spark higher interest and higher turnout, it is difficult to untangle the independent effect of advertising on rates of turnout. Likewise, if candidates in competitive races are more likely to use attack advertising, and if candidates in competitive races are by definition in electoral jeopardy, it becomes difficult to determine the effect of attack advertising on a candidate's share of the vote. In other words, one cannot simply look at the success rates of candidates who aired attack ads without considering the strategic context that encouraged them to air such ads.

Finally, and as mentioned earlier, 1998 candidates for the House and Senate spent the vast majority of their advertising dollars on advertisements that focused on policy issues rather than personal ones. There are significant differences in the tone of these two sets of ads. Nearly 1 in 10 of all House candidates' positive spots focused on personal issues, about two-thirds focused on policy issues, and almost 1 in 4 emphasized both. In contrast, most of the negative spots were designed to tear down the opponent's issues, with more than 1 in 5 attack ads dealing with personal issues.

CONCLUSION

Negative campaigning, particularly in the form of short televised attack ads, is thought to be both a growing epidemic and a scourge on our democracy. This chapter has shown that the strategic environment and the sponsor of the ads influence the nature and tone of advertising in congressional elections. More competitive contests are likely to have more attack advertising. Furthermore, there is a clear division of labor between candidates and parties, with parties much more likely to go on the attack.

Normatively, whether the amount of negative ads is big or small depends largely on one's expectations and on whether contrast ads should be seen as a form of negative campaigning. The mere fact that the candidates and their allies say nasty things about one another is by itself hardly a matter for much surprise or outrage. Some attack ads are a part of a broader effort to impart important and largely factual information to the electorate. These seem to us to be acceptable. Others, of course, mislead and twist and are much harder to defend. Our experience from reviewing several thousand ads was that attack ads were not always the most dishonest. Some of the biggest whoppers that we saw came in ads that promoted candidates; some of the most incisive and valuable information was imparted in attack and contrast ads.

The fact that negative ads are much more likely in competitive races is largely unsurprising given what we know about candidates' beliefs. It makes perfect sense that, if candidates think that attack ads work, they would be more prevalent in the tightest races where victory or defeat seem perilously close. All of the reasons not to go negative—starting with the potential damage to one's own reputation—are less and less relevant when a congressional seat hangs in the balance. Furthermore, close races help generate the sort of campaign war chests that make it possible for candidates and their allies to saturate the airwaves.

The glaring distinction between candidates' and parties' behavior, however, is a bit more of a surprise. Most observers of the 1998 election understood party TV ads as an extension of the candidates' efforts. The party ads raised many of the same issues and often used the same language and visuals as did the candidate ads. Despite the fact that the parties called their television advertisements "issue advocacy" ads, the commercials they ran were almost entirely oriented to helping individual candidates win elections. The parties' eagerness to help their candidates led them to do some of the dirtiest work in the campaign, taking on the tough chore of broadcasting attack ads to soften up the opposition. Whether this role helps build the sort of vigorous party-based system that many political scientists support is an open question, but one thing is certain: The rise of issue advocacy ads has given the parties a new, and somewhat negative, role to play in elections. For this reason, parties will continue to raise soft money and reformers will continue to press Congress to outlaw it.

APPENDIX

Two of the items that coders responded to are of particular interest here. First of all, after culling ads that related directly to state and/or local elections, we asked coders whether the remaining ads were intended to "generate support or opposition to a particular candidate" or to "provide information or urge action on other public policy issues." We used this question to distinguish between genuine issue ads and commercials with an obvious political purpose. There were many more examples of the second than of the first: Coders rated 95 percent of the ads broadcast as electioneering, compared with just 4 percent that were truly issue-focused and 1 percent whose intent was unclear. Our tests for intercoder reliability showed a high degree of agreement among coders, a source of some reassurance.

This item is reminiscent of the so-called "reasonable person" standard that the Federal Election Commission, other regulatory agencies, and various legislatures have attempted to codify in order to define the boundaries of the communications that fall under the jurisdiction of campaign finance

TABLE A-1   CODING THE TONE OF CAMPAIGN ADS (%)

	FAVORED CANDIDATE MENTIONED	OPPOSING CANDIDATE MENTIONED	BOTH CANDIDATES MENTIONED
Promote ad	97	0	8
Attack ad	1	100	16
Contrast ad	2	0	75
(N)	(136,935)	(63,650)	(74,951)

laws. Courts, however, have consistently rejected these attempts, claiming that reasonable person tests are vague and unworkable. The experience of our undergraduate coders, however, suggests there is much less confusion about assessing the underlying purpose of ads than judges seem to imagine.

We coded the tone of the ad with a simple question: "In your judgment, is the primary purpose of the ad to promote a specific candidate, to attack a candidate, or to contrast the candidate?" How accurate were the coders' decisions? Our reliability tests showed a high degree of agreement; commercials that appeared to one of our coders to be attack ads generally appeared to be attack ads to the others. Even more important, the coding protocol offers some internal evidence of the accuracy of responses to this simple question. Coders were also asked in separate items whether the ads mentioned the "favored candidate" and the "favored candidate's opponent." The relationship between these items and assessments of the tone of the ads was very close (see Table A-1). Nearly all of the ads that mentioned only one of the candidates ended up being rated as promote or attack ads, while three-quarters of the ads in which both candidates were featured were labeled as contrast ads. This is exactly the pattern one would expect from these items—a strong indication that coders understood the distinction between the three categories of ads they examined and were able to differentiate them accurately.

ACKNOWLEDGMENTS

Data for this project were obtained from the Brennan Center for Justice at New York University's School of Law, which acquired the data set with funding from The Pew Charitable Trusts. We thank the Brennan Center and the Pew Trusts. We thank Harley Ellenberger and Evan Tracey of Campaign Media Analysis Group for all that they have done to make this project possible. We take full responsibility for any errors we may have made in analyzing the data set.

NOTES

1. Gary C. Jacobson, "The Impact of Broadcast Campaigning on Electoral Outcomes," *The Journal of Politics* 37 (1975): 769–793; Gary C. Jacobson, "Money and Votes Reconsidered: Congressional Elections, 1972–1982," *Public Choice* 47 (1985): 7–62; Gary C. Jacobson, "The Effects of Campaign Spending in House Elections: New Evidence for Old Arguments," *American Journal of Political Science* 34 (1090): 334–362.
2. Kenneth Goldstein and Paul Freedman N.D., "New Evidence for New Arguments," forthcoming in *Journal of Politics*; Jonathan S. Krasno and Daniel E. Seltz, *Buying Time: Television Advertising in the 1998 Congressional Elections* (New York: Brennan Center for Justice, 2000); Paul S. Herrnson, *Congressional Elections: Campaigning at Home and in Washington*, 3rd ed. (Washington, DC: CQ Press, 2000), 228–243.
3. Steven Finkel and John Greer, "A Spot Check: Casting Doubt on the Demobilizing Effect of Attack Advertising," *American Journal of Political Science* 42 (1998): 573–595; Goldstein and Freedman, "New Evidence for New Arguments"; Martin P. Wattenberg and Craig Leonard Brians, "Negative Campaign Advertising: Demobilizer or Mobilizer?" *American Political Science Review* 93 (1999): 891–899.
4. Montague Kern, *30-Second Politics: Political Advertising in the 1980s* (New York: Praeger, 1989), 18.
5. Richard Lau, "Two Explanations for Negativity Effects in Political Behavior," *American Journal of Political Science* 29 (1985): 119–138.
6. Richard R. Lau, Lee Sigelman, Caroline Heldman, and Paul Babbitt, "The Effects of Negative Political Advertisements: A Meta-Analytic Assessment," *American Political Science Review* 93 (1999): 851–875.
7. Issue advocacy stems from footnote 42 of the Supreme Court's 1976 landmark ruling, *Buckley v. Valeo*, in which the Court limited application of the Federal Election Campaign Act (FECA) to communications which "expressed advocated" the election or defeat of a candidate by means of such phrases as "vote for," "vote against," "support," or "defeat." Subsequent rulings by lower courts have tended to interpret this footnote quite literally, creating a "magic words" standard dividing electioneering covered by FECA from nonelectoral issue speech which is not.
8. In 1998, the New York and Los Angeles media markets, which contain over 10 percent of all House seats, had few hotly contested races.
9. The coders were honors students in political science at Arizona State University.
10. Herrnson, *Congressional Elections*, 193, 200.
11. Glen Moramacaro, *Regulatory Electioneering* (New York: Brennan Center for Justice, 1998).
12. Advertisers argue that any communication that omits the magic words of express advocacy is not electioneering and therefore not subject to federal campaign finance laws (see note 7). This allows them to avoid disclosing their receipts and expenditures as candidates do, plus it gives them the opportunity to raise money in unlimited amounts from donors, including corporations and labor unions.
13. One indication of the importance that the candidates attach to the moral high ground was the amount of debate between George Bush and John McCain early in 2000 over campaign tactics—which side ran the first attack ad, who was running a nastier campaign, and so on.

14. David Magleby, *Outside Money: Soft Money and Issue Advocacy in the 1998 Congressional Elections* (Lanham, MD: Rowlan and Littlefield, 2000).

15. American Political Science Association, "Toward a More Responsible Two-Party System," *American Political Science Review* 44, Supplement (1950): 15–36, 37–84, 488–499.

16. The 1979 amendments to FECA allowed parties exceptions to the rules on raising and spending money for party building, a phrase that at the time literally meant brick-and-mortar buildings and carrying out voter mobilization drives and other grass-roots efforts. Subsequently, party building grew to include non-candidate-focused generic party advertisements and, more recently, issue advocacy advertisements that focused on individual candidates and campaigns.

17. Charles Cook, *The Cook Report*, October 20, 1998.

18. Michael Barone, *Almanac of American Politics* (Web Edition, 2000). http://national journal.com/members/campaign/1998/

19. Barone, *Almanac of American Politics*.

20. *Las Vegas Review*, November 4, 1998.

21. Barone, *Almanac of American Politics*.

22. Barone, *Almanac of American Politics*.

23. Kim Fridkin Kahn and Patrick J. Kenney, *The Spectacle of U.S. Senate Campaigns* (Princeton, NJ: Princeton University Press, 1999), 74–98.

6

CAMPAIGN STRATEGY
AND DIRECT VOTER CONTACT

MICHAEL T. HANNAHAN

Politicians are in the business of persuasion. They try to persuade people to support them and, when voters are favorably disposed toward their campaigns, politicians try to motivate them to come out and vote. Victorious politicians spend much of their tenure trying to convince colleagues to support this or that piece of legislation, while defeated politicians wade into the most difficult of streams and attempt to persuade their supporters to retire the debt left over from a losing campaign. One of the oldest, and still one of the most common, persuasion tools in the political tool kit is direct voter contact.

Direct voter contact refers to that portion of the campaign that uses techniques to reach out to individual voters. Despite how it may appear, many campaign activities target groups of voters rather than individuals. For example, while an individual voter experiences television and radio at home, or maybe in the car on the way to work, the commercial is targeted at a demographic group, not an individual. Because commercials typically target a group and are then broadcast over the airways, people outside of the target audience also receive the message. Direct contact is often contrasted with "broadcasting" and is sometimes even referred to as "narrowcasting" by consultants because it only reaches its intended audience.

Direct voter contact was the only method of political communication before radio and television. Roman elections were conducted using written endorsements and campaign posters. American campaigns in the nineteenth century and early twentieth century were arenas for intense partisan get-out-the-vote (GOTV) efforts characterized by emotional rallies and marches. Modern campaigns have television and radio available to them but still devote substantial resources to direct contact efforts. The modern version of direct contact relies more on using computers to generate target lists of specific voters, pretested messages designed to persuade voters, and telephone, mail, or door-to-door activities to deliver those messages. However, the basic principal remains the same—to communicate a compelling message directly to an individual voter.

This chapter explores the role of direct voter contact in contemporary elections by examining the strategies of eight recent campaigns for the U.S. House of Representatives. It also analyzes the impact voter contact has had on voter turnout and electoral outcomes. Finally, it explores some important normative questions about the role of direct contact in the campaign system. Because direct contact increases voter turnout and is targeted at specific groups of voters, it has significant implications for voter participation in elections and for campaign reform.

Campaign Strategy and Direct Contact

Maryland's 5th congressional district covers three rural counties in southern Maryland, as well as large parts of suburban Prince George's and Anne Arundel Counties. This district usually produces a Republican challenger strong enough to raise money and attract attention but not strong enough to win. In 1992 Democratic congressman Steny Hoyer, then in his sixth full term in the House, faced Republican Lawrence Hogan Jr. in a contest thought by many observers to be one of the most interesting in the nation.

Hoyer's professional campaign team was headed by a general consultant from New Mexico named Chris Brown. Brown devised a voter identification and GOTV program for the 5th district. In a series of meetings with campaign staff and other professionals, Brown laid out his plan. Approximately 50,000 people were targeted based on their party affiliation, voting history, and demographic characteristics. The goal was to identify as many favorable and undecided voters in swing precincts as possible.

The actual telephone calls were made by an Oregon firm named Telemark. Voter names and numbers came from an electronic voter file compiled from original county tapes. Voter Contact Services (VCS), a firm with offices in Hawaii, California, and Massachusetts, provided the data and the computer work. The voter file contained the names of 280,000 registered voters, initially all of those in the 5th district. It contained each individual's history of voter turnout dating back to the 1988 primary and general elections, their birth date, gender, party affiliation, precinct, telephone number, ethnicity, housing prices, educational levels, and other information about the geographical areas in which they resided. VCS used combinations of these variables to create a "target file" of 50,000 voters. Telemark used computer-assisted dialing technology to call these voters to determine their partisanship and voting intentions. VCS added this information to the Hoyer voter file and used it to determine which voters the campaign would directly contact. Mailing tapes and labels were generated for these voters and sent to various direct-mail houses around the country. The mail houses were responsible for producing and mailing the Hoyer campaign's voter contact mail. A few days before the election, lists of favorable voters were sent back to Telemark, which made telephone calls to mobilize Hoyer's supporters.

The Maryland race involved consultants and personnel in seven states across five time zones. The Hoyer campaign spent $1,584,271 on all campaign activities in 1992, while challenger Hogan spent a total of $265,065. In 1994 the Hoyer campaign repeated, on a smaller scale, the voter contact program described above. The 1992 data were moved forward and matched to a new voter file so that the process might be repeated more efficiently in the 1994 and 1996 elections.

This example illustrates that direct contact thrives on the use of technical and professional resources to reach specific voter targets. Indeed, the strength of direct mail is its ability to reach individual voters with a specific message. Targeting and its associated benefits are at the heart of direct contact's appeal to campaigns. Cost is also important, and direct mail is cheaper than other forms of campaign communication, especially television. Well-funded campaigns waged by presidential, senatorial, gubernatorial, and many congressional candidates consider television the most important advertising medium, but direct contact still makes up a significant budgetary item in these races.[1] Less expensive campaigns, including most races for state legislative seats, county posts, and municipal offices, make direct contact their major means of communication, spending little if any money on television advertising. If the budgets of all election campaigns were combined, direct contact, including telephone calls and mail, might well be the largest area of campaign spending in the nation.[2]

COSTS OF DIRECT CONTACT

In 1994 congressional campaigns spent a grand total of $302,250,996. Of that, $51,728,222 (17 percent) was spent on GOTV and $32,326,643 (12 percent) went to direct mail, for a combined direct contact percentage of 28 percent. As might be expected, the variation in spending for direct contact was quite wide. Direct-mail expenditures ranged from $3,300 to $662,700. The typical campaign spends an average of 12 percent of its budget on direct mail.

Candidates in urban areas considered direct contact to be more important to their campaign than television, whereas their more rural counterparts had the opposite experience.[3] In many urban districts the electronic media markets are very expensive because they broadcast to millions of viewers, most of whom live outside the district. Time purchased on Los Angeles television costs approximately $814 per rating point and reaches well beyond the 30th congressional district, whereas a candidate in the 3rd congressional district of

Ohio would pay about $75 per point and would mainly reach 3rd district voters. TV would be useful to candidates in both districts, but affordable for candidates in only one. Expensive channels are inefficient as well. Urban areas like New York City and Los Angeles are perhaps the best example of the inefficiency of advertising with television, but adjoining states also fall victim to expensive media markets. New Jersey relies almost entirely on New York and Philadelphia television. Whenever a candidate puts on a television ad in South Jersey, all of Philadelphia sees it. More people who live outside of the district view the candidate's ad than voters within the district. As a result, direct mail is more efficient for many campaigns than the electronic media because it can be used to target voters in one and only one district.

Moreover, its advantages in targeting, message delivery, and cost make direct contact an indispensable component of most House campaigns, including those with high expenditures on television. In fact, spending on television and direct contact are correlated: The more a campaign spends on TV, the more it spends on direct contact.[4]

CAMPAIGN STRATEGY

Campaign decision making is at the intersection of art and science. Quantitative data analysis and computerized methods often guide how things are done. Consultant salesmanship, talents, and tastes usually decide what things are done. When campaign decision makers believe that direct mail is more effective than television or that the message is more efficiently communicated by using a variety of channels, they invest more in direct mail. As in most industries, decisions are based on past results, personal relationships, reputation, and trust. These considerations are important, but they take a back seat to costs. Direct voter contact is more prevalent than TV in House campaigns because it is sometimes a cheaper and more efficient way to reach voters.

Once a campaign decides on a course of direct contact, the voter file becomes its most important technical resource. Voter targeting is constrained by three factors: the imagination of the consultant, money, and data. A consultant's imagination is the least limiting factor. Money, or lack thereof, however, limits every aspect of campaigning. Complex targeting often requires matching expensive data files containing information about individuals and their neighborhoods to the voter file. Finally, targeting is constrained by the amount and type of data available in the voter file. List vending firms, like VCS, compile voter files from official county or state voter registration files. At best, government voter files contain name, address, party affiliation, birth date, registration date, gender, ethnicity, and past voting history. Some list vendors include additional information such as local housing values and estimated income. Past voting history and party affiliation are the most important of these variables in political targeting.

Campaign advertising is part of an overall communications system. In this system, voter habits and expectations combine with current media and computer technology to determine the mix of campaign communication methods and messages. All campaign communications begin with a target group and a message, which are central to the campaign's strategy. What is said, how it is said, and to whom it is said make up the bulk of critical campaign decisions. Targeting and message development have become so sophisticated that one consultant has developed some general rules about the impact that the colors used in direct-mail pieces have on voter impressions of the campaign.[5]

There are four important facets to direct contact: purpose, message, delivery method, and source. Source refers to the origin of the contact. The two most important factors here are the party of the candidate and whether the candidate is an incumbent or a challenger. Examples drawn from eight campaigns waged in Maryland's 5th, Ohio's 1st, California's 1st, and Pennsylvania's 21st congressional districts are used to illustrate these. The Maryland and Ohio races are from 1994, and the Pennsylvania and California contests are from 1996. They allow us to examine direct contact in presidential and off-year elections. The California and Maryland races were in expensive television markets, whereas the Ohio and Pennsylvania districts were in lower-cost areas, allowing us to compare the impact that TV advertising costs have on campaign strategy.

TARGETING

Targeting is one of the distinguishing features of modern campaigns. Campaign strategists use voters' partisanship and voting history to divide the electorate into friends, foes, and persuadables. Friends receive messages encouraging them to vote, foes are ignored, and the persuadables are targeted by both campaigns, making them the beneficiaries of a lively battle for their affections. Voter targeting is both a cause and effect of a volatile electorate, candidate-centered campaigns, and voters accustomed to sophisticated communication technology.

Targeting is used to accomplish three objectives: to persuade voters, to urge voters to the polls, or to identify how voters feel about a candidate or an issue. Although all three purposes are achieved by similar techniques, they are different enough to have spawned separate industries. Persuasion efforts rely heavily on the mail and are managed by direct-mail firms. Turnout and voter identification programs are usually telephone or door-to-door efforts. The world of turnout and voter identification is more diverse than the persuasion universe. Campaign volunteers, party workers, professional phone banks, and field consultants all perform the necessary technical tasks.

Turnout efforts tend to include more volunteers than persuasion direct contact techniques, but it is always possible for a campaign to use volunteers for the production and delivery of mail. It also is common for professional telephone centers to make GOTV calls. Persuasion telephone calls and mailings are both designed to affect turnout, but the distinction between the two is important to remember.

The 1994 telephoning efforts of then Democratic incumbent David Mann provide an example of both turnout and persuasion efforts. Running in Ohio's 1st congressional district against a well-funded opponent, Mann used the relatively cheap Cincinnati TV market to communicate the bulk of his message. Direct contact was used to get Democrats to vote. Increasing Democratic turnout was critical to the Mann strategy because Democrats formed a majority of the voters in the district. The campaign made two telephone efforts. Their pollster, Penn and Schoen, designed a turnout program aimed at Democratic voters. The telephone script read, "David Mann needs your vote. Please turn out on Tuesday. Your polling place is (name of polling place)." Blue Chip Marketing, a Cincinnati-based telemarketing firm, called selected precincts with a more detailed persuasion message. The caller asked to speak with a particular voter, praised Mann's record in Congress, and urged the voter to participate in the election on the following Tuesday. The Blue Chip calls went to independents who lived in Democratic areas—voters the campaign felt could be moved toward Mann with the right message.

MESSAGE

No good campaign communicates with voters without having first defined a message. The mix of campaign messages is determined by the candidate's party, status, and public opinion research. Status refers to whether or not a candidate is an incumbent, a challenger, or a contestant for an open seat. Party and incumbency are the most important strategic dimensions of campaign planning and the two most important voter information shortcuts.[6] Candidates focus on their records and emphasize issues that are viewed favorably by voters.[7] Incumbents have an advantage because they are often the only candidates in a race who have a record of any sort. Incumbent David Mann in Ohio's 1st congressional district sent out a collection of newspaper headlines praising his work. Incumbent Frank Riggs in California's 1st congressional district sent out a collection of newspaper endorsements and a piece highlighting his environmental record.

Candidates may also emphasize issues already identified with their party.[8] In 1994 the "Contract with America" provided a ready identification for Republican candidates. Republicans are usually associated with crime and taxes, whereas Democrats are often seen as more capable of handling education and Social Security. The content and quantity of issues is also affected by the competitiveness of the race. As the race becomes closer the messages become more negative.[9] Noncompetitive races are characterized by a comparable lack of campaign information.[10] Incumbents are more likely to send positive messages highlighting their background, while challengers are more likely to attack the incumbent.[11]

The exact content of campaign messages varies greatly, but it is common to divide them into negative attacks, positive communications, and issue pieces.[12] Negative attacks shine an unflattering light on one's opponent or offer an enlightening comparison between the two candidates to the disadvantage of one's rival. Despite its reputation, not all negative communication is "dirty." Voters deserve to know about candidate weaknesses as well as candidate strengths.[13]

The 1996 race in California's 1st congressional district exemplifies this. This highly competitive district is north of San Francisco and very distinct from the Bay Area. Despite the cultural differences, most of the 1st congressional district falls within the San Francisco media market. Because television is expensive, campaigns often turn to direct mail to convey messages. Incumbent Republican Frank Riggs used 13 pieces of mail to create a positive picture of his record and a negative view of the challenger, Angela Alioto. The negative mailings were large, graphic pieces. The outer portion of the mailings conveyed the message with a picture and a headline. One negative mailing, called "Her Heart," implied that Alioto, a San Francisco native who had moved to the district to run for office, had left her heart in her native city. A second attack, called "Little People," detailed taxes that the wealthy Alioto had failed to pay on time and contrasted that with a statement that "People who can afford to pay their taxes should be happy to pay their taxes." The final attack piece was sent to a group of voters the campaign had identified as "persuadable." Entitled "Bothered," it summarized the other attacks with three lines: "She can't be bothered to pay taxes; she can't be bothered to vote; she can't be bothered to live here." All of the mailings featured large black-and-white photos. One showed Alioto's San Francisco home. Another was a picture of her luxurious new residence. All of the pieces were designed to give even the most casual reader the impression that Alioto was an out-of-touch carpetbagger.

Like negative communications, positive communications have a personal emphasis that is not always directly related to public policy. A positive image message emphasizes personal experience, history, and accomplishments. A typical positive piece might be used to improve name identification; it will describe the candidate in positive, memorable terms, which will have a strong resonance with the voters in a particular district. In the 1996 race for Pennsylvania's 21st district House seat, for example, Democratic challenger Ron DiNicola was attacked by Republican incumbent Phil English for being an out-of-state lawyer. DiNicola responded with a mail piece called "Bricklayer." This mailing sought to redefine DiNicola from the slick Hollywood lawyer portrayed by the English campaign to an ex-marine who epitomized the local boy made good. The tag line was "Tough enough to box in the Marines, smart enough to go to Harvard." It also reminded voters that he had been born in the district to an Italian immigrant bricklayer. That piece was mailed to the union and Democratic voters in Butler and Mercer Counties. It showed the importance placed on winning the votes of likely supporters.

Campaigns also communicate with voters about issues. Issue communications present a candidate's stand on substantive public policy questions. The English–DiNicola race was one of the 20 closest House races in the country. English barely prevailed, winning by fewer than 1,000 votes despite outspending DiNicola $1,262,645 to $478,871. Both campaigns knew that the senior vote was critical because the district has one of the highest percentages of senior citizen voters in the nation. English sent two mailings to senior citizens. The first piece contained a signed letter from the very popular former congressman and current governor of Pennsylvania, Tom Ridge. In the letter Ridge defended English's efforts on behalf of Social Security:

> Phil English realizes that Pennsylvania has the second highest senior population in America.... When it comes to Medicare and Social Security, Phil's position is crystal clear; you earned it, you deserve it, you were promised it, you are counting on it, and he will make sure you get it.[14]

The second mailing sent to seniors throughout the district consisted of a simple oversized postcard with a picture of a senior citizen and the headline "No one has worked harder for us than Phil English."

For his part DiNicola sent direct mail to all Democratic and independent voters who were 65 or over and lived in Butler County. The campaign called this the "Older Voter/FDR" piece. It emphasized DiNicola's ties to traditional Democratic issues as well as the threat Republicans presented to the elderly by contrasting Democratic support for Social Security with "Republican attacks on our most important social program." Both candidates tried to reassure senior voters that they were fully behind the current Social Security system.

MESSAGE DELIVERY

The campaign message forms part of the strategic framework for campaign direct contact. There are also tactical choices involved in all campaign communication efforts. The most basic involve choosing among different media, such as television, radio, or direct contact. More refined choices include selection among different types of voter contact, including mail, telephone, and door-to-door efforts. Campaigns often use all three methods of direct contact. Challenger Steve Chabot, who was in a close race in Ohio's 1st congressional district, used a comprehensive precinct leader program that integrated all three. A volunteer found 80 families in each of 200 key precincts that were willing to have their picture taken with Chabot and printed on a postcard. The text on the reverse side of the card was precinct specific and said something like "We live on Elm Street and we are another *Family for Steve Chabot*." The postcards were mailed to voters living in the vicinity of the nearest family. Approximately 30,000 postcards were mailed to registered Republicans and independents residing in 120 precincts. These same voters also were contacted through door-to-door walking efforts and GOTV phone calls.

MESSAGE RECIPIENTS

Strategic campaigns develop a message that they deliver to a limited set of voters using a variety of techniques. This begs the question: Which voters receive direct contacts? What impact do these contacts have?

Ohio's 1st, Maryland's 5th, California's 1st, and Pennsylvania's 21st congressional districts have a total of 1.36 million voters. I used a data set that records all of the direct contacts made by the Democratic and Republican candidates' campaigns in these districts to examine the types of contacts used to reach specific voters. Ninety-five percent of the voters in these four districts received at least 1 contact from at least 1 candidate. Sixty-six percent of these individuals voted on Election Day. The eight campaigns made 4,838,297 attempts to directly contact individual voters—an average of 604,787 contacts per campaign, or a little more than 2 contacts per campaign per voter.

Most consultants believe that a message must be received several times before it registers in a voter's mind. One rule of thumb suggests that a television buy needs a minimum of 300 Gross Rating Points (GRP) before any kind of voter movement is to be expected. Three hundred GRP's indicate that the commercial is seen by the target audience 3 times. Many consultants feel that the "rule of three" applies to messages received through direct contact as well. Voters can be divided into those who receive a low level of direct contact (less than 3 contacts), a moderate level (between 3 and 5 total contacts), and a high level (more than 5 contacts). The average voter in Ohio's 1st district received 2.53 contacts and falls into the first group. The average voter in California's 1st district was contacted 6.89 times and belongs in the last group.

Approximately half of the voters in Ohio and Pennsylvania received fewer than 3 contacts, while 80 percent and 87 percent of the voters in Maryland and California respectively received more than 3 contacts (see Table 6-1). Direct contact was a more attractive option in Maryland and California because there are substantially higher TV costs there than in Ohio and Pennsylvania.

The distribution of campaign contacts is just as important as the number of contacts. Older voters, habitual voters, and registered party members receive more direct contact than young voters, infrequent voters, and registered independents (see Table 6-2). Most campaigns pursue the dual strategy of courting their base—those voters whose partisanship, ideology, and background predispose them to support the candidate—and undecided voters. Challenger DiNicola in Pennsylvania's 21st congressional district spent the

TABLE 6-1   THE DISTRIBUTION OF DIRECT VOTER CONTACTS (%)

	CALIFORNIA	MARYLAND	OHIO	PENNSYLVANIA
Low	12.7	21.0	51.3	53.0
Moderate	24.3	44.5	34.5	39.0
High	62.6	35.0	18.6	8.0
Total Contacts	296,316	265,192	272,186	302,991

Note: Figures represent percentages of voters receiving low, moderate, or high numbers of contacts.

TABLE 6-2   THE IMPACT OF AGE, PARTY,
AND ELECTORAL PARTICIPATION ON VOTER CONTACT

	MARYLAND	OHIO	PENNSYLVANIA	CALIFORNIA	ALL FOUR STATES
Age					
18–25	4.3	2.00	1.9	5.7	3.70
26–35	4.5	2.30	2.0	6.2	3.90
36–45	4.3	2.40	2.0	6.6	4.00
46–55	4.4	2.50	2.0	6.5	4.30
56–65	4.5	2.70	2.7	8.3	4.90
65 plus	4.5	3.00	5.1	8.0	5.90
Party					
Republican	7.1	2.90	2.8	7.6	4.90
Democrat	3.1	0.86	2.7	6.0	4.30
Independent	2.7	3.00	1.2	6.3	3.70
Voting History					
0 elections	4.0	1.96	2.1	6.1	4.02
1 elections	4.3	1.69	2.5	5.8	3.96
2 elections	4.6	3.43	2.6	7.9	4.77
3 elections	5.0	2.50	2.8	7.7	4.91
4 elections	5.0	2.60	3.0	7.0	5.01

Note: Figures represent the mean number of campaign contacts received by members of each voting group.

majority of his campaign resources on union and Democratic households, which comprise his voter base. Incumbent Frank Riggs, by contrast, needed to persuade large blocks of undecided voters to support his candidacy and sent many issue mailings to groups of independent voters. Most campaigns target their base and persuadable voters, but some raid their opponent's base.[15]

Decisions about exactly which base and undecided voters to contact involve strategic and budgetary considerations. The strategic element in targeting focuses on getting the right message into the right hands, and the budgetary element looks to save scarce resources by directing contacts to likely voters. Party affiliation and age are often important considerations. Party members vote at higher rates than do nonparty members. Campaigns can usually count on members of their party to support them. High turnout levels and partisan loyalty make partisans major targets of direct voter contact. For that reason, challenger Donald Devine in Maryland's 5th congressional district sent seven mailings to registered Republicans in an attempt to solidify his base of loyal supporters. Campaigns also contact older voters more frequently than younger ones. Age figures into issue mailings because older citizens are interested in Social Security, a program that has provided more than its share of partisan conflict over the years. Democrats routinely accuse Republicans of wanting to gut Social Security, and Republicans routinely respond with assertions along the lines of Phil Gramm's, "Ah would nevah cut my momma's check." Challenger Steve Chabot in Ohio's 1st congressional district also needed to defend himself against Democratic attacks on his Social Security policy. He mailed a piece to all seniors in his district that pictured him standing with his mother and promising never to cut Medicare. Older citizens are also targeted because they are very likely to vote. Thus, older voters are heavily targeted because of their issue concerns and propensity to vote.

The effects of age, party affiliation, and past voting behavior sometimes overlap and cancel each other out. For example, Donald Devine's campaign focused on mailing to Republican voters regardless of their age and voting history. Phil English, in Pennsylvania's 21st congressional district, mailed campaign literature to all seniors regardless of their voting history or party affiliation. Even though campaigns do not always target populations based on age, voting history, and party affiliation at the same time, one or more of these factors usually influence their targeting decisions.

Older voters, who are the most likely to vote, receive more contacts from campaigns than do younger voters (see Table 6-2). The number of contacts increases gradually from one age group to the next, but the difference between the youngest group and the oldest is more than two full contacts. Less dramatic but still noticeable are the differences between party and voting history. Independents are contacted less frequently than are either Republicans or Democrats because they have lower turnout rates and are not automatically considered part of a campaign's base; thus they are not the subject of broad-based GOTV efforts.

The case of voting history is more complex. People who voted in 4 elections receive nearly 1 additional contact, on average, than those who did not previously vote. Most of the difference is between nonvoters and individuals who voted in 2 or more elections. In fact, the mean number of contacts tends to peak with voters who voted in 2 elections. This nonlinear relationship highlights the tension involved when using voter history for targeting purposes. The more selective the targeting, the fewer people the campaign will reach. If, for example, a campaign strategist wanted to make sure a piece of mail went to likely voters and selected only those people who had voted in 5 of the last 5 elections, the odds of the campaign reaching likely voters will be very high, but it won't reach very many voters in total. Targeting based on voting history is a mix of reaching the right voters and reaching a large enough universe to win. The campaigns in California's 1st and Pennsylvania's 21st congressional districts debated whether to target voters who had voted in 1 of 3 or 2 of 3 of the last three general elections. If those voting in 1 of the last 3 were targeted, the number of individuals who received mail would have increased but the percentage of those people who were likely voters might have declined. Likewise, if those voting in 2 of the last 3 were targeted, the number of individuals contacted would have declined but the mail would have found its way into the hands of more likely voters. In the California race, both campaigns used the more restrictive approach, contacting two-election voters, to save money. In Pennsylvania, the Democratic campaign targeted a universe of voters who participated in at least 1 out of the last 3 general elections in order to get their message out to more voters and encourage them to support DiNicola.

Campaigns weigh strategic considerations differently. In Maryland, the Republican campaign chose to work almost exclusively on its base of registered Republicans, ignoring age and voting history. In Pennsylvania, where labor unions were targeting a freshman Republican and Social Security was a major issue, both candidates' targeting priorities focused on age. Voters over 65 were, on average, contacted 4 times more often than voters under 25. In California, where both campaigns sent out many highly targeted direct-mail pieces, older voters and voters with strong histories of voting received more contacts. In Ohio, with most of the efforts dictated by the district's geography, there is a flatter pattern among all the variables because all of the different demographic groups within each precinct received a similar number of contacts.

Campaign strategy, budgetary concerns, and tactical considerations combine to result in most voter contacts being concentrated among habitual voters—citizens who already are most likely to vote. Those least likely to vote—young, infrequent voters (and nonvoters) who are registered independents—are the least likely to receive direct mail from a campaign or a call encouraging them to vote. The question remains whether or not this disparity makes any difference and whether voter contact increases turnout.

THE EFFECTS OF DIRECT CONTACT

Voting is not an easy act to explain. The costs of voting often outweigh the potential benefits, especially in a large electorate where the chance of one vote affecting the outcome is small.[16] People may vote out of a sense of civic duty.

They may feel guilty about not voting or they may simply cast their vote out of habit.[17] In addition, some people may feel as if they have a greater stake in the political system than others. Citizens' attitudes toward politics, particularly their sense of political efficacy—their beliefs about their ability to influence the government—are positively related to voter turnout.[18] Differences in age, income, and education are reflected in differences in turnout rates.

Campaigns cannot alter the demographic characteristics of the electorate, but they can influence citizens' attitudes toward an election by providing voters with political information. Direct contact makes it easier for voters to understand campaigns by reminding them about an upcoming election and providing the information needed for a quick comparison of the two candidates running for office.[19] Equipped with this information, voters may feel that they are more important to the political process.[20] More important to campaign strategists is their belief that there is a relationship between campaign communications and voter turnout.

Whether it is through increasing citizens' stock of political knowledge or by improving their sense of political efficacy, direct voter contact does have a significant impact on voter turnout even when one controls for party, age, and past voting history (see Table 6-3). In Maryland, a voter who was contacted 3 or more times by a campaign was 6 percent more likely to turn out than a voter who had not been contacted at all. In Pennsylvania that figure is 3 percent, while in California the increase in turnout stands at 9.7 percent. In the Ohio district, direct contact did not appear to have any impact on turnout.

Age and voting history are also directly related to voter turnout. Sixty-year-olds are more likely to vote than 25-year-olds. Past voting history has the strongest impact on future voting. In all four districts, people who had already participated in at least two elections were 35 percent more likely to vote than those who hadn't voted at all. In contrast, the effects of total contacts and party affiliation are more varied. The effects of age and voting

TABLE 6-3   THE EFFECTS OF DIRECT CONTACT ON VOTER TURNOUT (%)

	OHIO	MARYLAND	PENNSYLVANIA	CALIFORNIA	ALL FOUR STATES
Total Contacts	—	6.0	3.0	9.7	4.0
Voting History	37.0	39.0	31.0	34.0	35.0
Age	11.0	7.0	6.0	3.0	5.5
Democrat	22.0	–.7	—	–1.4	3.6
Republican	29.0	—	5.3	6.5	7.3

Note: Partial effects represent changes in the probability of voting as follows: Total Contacts = change from 0 to 3 contacts; Voting History = change from voting in 0 elections to voting in 2 elections; Age = a comparison between a 25-year-old voter and a 60-year-old voter; Democrat and Republican = the change in probability compared with an independent voter. — = Not significant. For more information see the full model in the Appendix.

history are fairly consistent across the United States. Sixty-year-olds are part of an age cohort that share a common history. Likewise, habitual voters are more likely to vote in current elections than are nonvoters, no matter where they live. The effect of direct contact, however, varies. Campaigns use diverse strategies and devote different amounts of resources to persuading and turning out voters. Campaigns that spend more on direct contact typically stimulate greater voter turnout.

Direct contact had a stronger effect on infrequent voters than on habitual voters in every race but the one in Ohio, where the effects of contacts were insignificant (see Table 6-4). In the other three elections, the contacts had no significant effect on the probability of turnout among habitual voters, but they had a big impact on infrequent voters. In Maryland, infrequent voters who were contacted 3 times were nearly 7 percent more likely to vote than were those who were not contacted. In Pennsylvania, the probability of turnout among infrequent voters increased by 5.6 percent with the addition of 3 contacts. California showed the greatest difference with the receipt of 3 contacts, increasing the probability that an infrequent voter would turn out by more than 13 percent.

Different methods of direct contact have different effects on voters. Telephones, for example, work better at increasing turnout than does mail, which is designed primarily to persuade voters. The Hoyer campaign's telephone efforts increased the turnout of the voters it targeted. The campaign first identified independent voters as supporters or persuadable voters. Then, it called Hoyer's supporters twice a few days before the election to remind them to vote for the congressman. The independents who were identified as persuadable voters were called with a persuasive message that highlighted Hoyer's accomplishments in office. Multiple telephone calls appear to work better than a single call. In California's 1st district, a number of Democrats

TABLE 6-4   THE CHANGE IN THE PROBABILITY OF VOTING FOR HABITUAL
AND INFREQUENT VOTERS DUE TO VOTER CONTACT (%)

STATE VOTING HABITS	MEAN	NO CONTACTS	THREE CONTACTS
Ohio Infrequent Voters	37.7	—	—
Ohio Habitual Voters	82.7	—	—
Maryland Infrequent Voters	38.3	28.8	35.5
Maryland Habitual Voters	89.7	—	—
Pennsylvania Infrequent Voters	48.3	44.1	49.7
Pennsylvania Habitual Voters	87.7	—	—
California Infrequent Voters	51.8	24.1	37.3
California Habitual Voters	91.9	—	—

Note: Figures represent the probability of voting at each age and contact range. The mean represents the probability of turnout while holding all variables at their mean. The model controls for age, voting history, party, and total contacts. Constants are included in each model. — = Not significant. All other figures are significant at the .05 level. For more information see the full model in the Appendix.

received just one call urging them to vote from challenger Alioto's campaign, but this effort led to no appreciable increase in turnout.

Door-to-door efforts do not appear to have a positive impact on voter turnout. In Pennsylvania's 21st district, challenger DiNicola's staff devised a comprehensive door-to-door effort in cooperation with labor unions. Union and other volunteer campaign workers knocked on the doors of Democrats with infrequent voting records in an effort to get them to the polls, but to little effect. Either because the effort was not well constructed or because the people were simply not interested in voting, the door-to-door campaign did not increase voter turnout above expected levels.

The content and source of direct mail is also important. Positive character pieces and negative attacks offer more opportunities for presenting dramatic information than do issue communications. Both candidates in California's 1st district relied heavily on direct mail to communicate both their positive and negative messages. Alioto attacked Congressman Riggs's record on gun control in a mail piece that showed a pair of gloved hands holding an automatic weapon. The piece implied that Riggs allowed dangerous weapons to fall into the wrong hands. Riggs countered with a barrage of mail that portrayed Alioto as an out-of-touch carpetbagger running against an incumbent with a long record of district service. In Pennsylvania's 1st district, DiNicola attacked English on his Social Security record, but English, as the incumbent, had the luxury of responding by mailing out his actual votes on the issue. Both examples support the generalization that incumbents' direct-mail pieces usually have a more significant impact than do challengers'. Voters appear to respond more positively to the familiar communications they receive from the "devil" they know than the unfamiliar communications they receive from the "devil" they don't.

CONCLUSION

Campaign direct contact efforts can increase voter turnout. Campaigns target most of their direct contact efforts on habitual voters, but, ironically, voter contact has the greatest impact on individuals who are infrequent voters. Of special note are the utility of repeated contacts and telephone calls in increasing turnout among younger, infrequent voters. Campaign strategists seeking to increase voter turnout should contact voters 3 or more times, preferably using the telephone. The targeting of habitual voters is built into the budgetary and strategic constraints faced by political campaigns. The concentration of political information into the hands of those already likely to participate is the direct contact equivalent of sending charitable contributions to Bill Gates or Donald Trump. This suggests that one way to attack low voter turnout is to alter the financial and strategic situations faced by political campaigns to encourage them to distribute their voter contact resources to more citizens.

Campaign finance reforms that attempt to limit campaign spending or make fund-raising more difficult by tightening donation limits will make it more difficult for campaigns to use direct voter contact. A recently approved Massachusetts initiative imposes a spending cap on state representative districts of $30,000 ($18,000 for the primary, where there are almost no races, and $12,000 for the general election). To telephone each of the households within a Massachusetts state representative district a single time costs $20,000. To send each household in that same district a letter would cost approximately $17,000. Even if a campaign placed all $30,000 into direct contact efforts, assuming that a campaign could be run without a paid manager, lawyer, or accountant, that campaign could not send two pieces of mail or make two telephone calls to district voters. It might be possible to reduce the cost of direct contact by using volunteers; however, this would reinforce the already overwhelming strength of incumbents, who already have a core group of volunteers in place. Limitations on campaign spending and fund-raising could make it difficult for candidates, especially nonincumbents, to use multiple direct contacts to increase voter turnout.

Many political observers and journalists focus on campaign mudslinging and slight the potentially positive effects of campaign communications. This leads them to suggest that too much is spent on campaigns and that increased public control is required. Considering campaigns from an opposing perspective—as enterprises that form a useful part of our democratic system—supports making campaign communications resources, especially the tools of direct contact, more available because of the potential to increase voter turnout. Reforms aimed at limiting campaign spending will benefit incumbents and reduce turnout. An alternative approach to reform is warranted.

How can we encourage the use of direct contact to produce increased turnout and electoral change? Reformers seeking to promote the best use of political resources might consider reducing postage costs to encourage campaigns to use mail, using financial incentives, or even using government agencies to increase the number of election-day GOTV calls. They also might advocate that the voter information contained in voter contact files be made readily available to all candidates. The original goal of soft money—money spent outside federal limits, disclosure requirements, and other regulations by party organizations and interest groups—was to encourage the use of volunteers to increase voter participation and turnout. Instead of legislation that bans soft money, it might make more sense to make sure that soft money is directed toward its initial purpose.

Modern campaigns take place in a deafening arena. Because of the number of McDonald's ads appearing on television, my son's third and fourth words were "french fry." How do campaigns, with their comparatively minor resources, expended in a compressed time frame, get heard above the din? Recent trends in communication make it even more difficult for campaigns to be heard. The increased number of television stations, the Internet, telephone "caller ID," and the overwhelming influx of mail into our boxes combine to make the citizen more and more difficult to reach.

Direct contact increases turnout and may be the most effective tool politicians have at their disposal to promote the habit of voting throughout the electorate.[21] It is possible that political skeptics are accurate and that the content of campaign communication is often empty and misleading, but it is information nonetheless. There are tools that politicians can use to encourage greater citizen participation. Reformers should spend less effort trying to make it difficult for politicians to raise the money needed to obtain those tools and more time structuring a system that encourages politicians to use them to encourage both habitual and infrequent voters to go to the polls.

APPENDIX

The data were analyzed using logistic regression because the dependent variable, whether an individual voted or not, is dichotomous. Each model included a variable for the total number of contacts, age, past voting history, and party affiliation (see Tables A-1 and A-2). The partial effects in Tables 6-3 and 6-4 represent the increase in voting probability over the base category of independent.

TABLE A-1   THE IMPACT OF AGE, VOTING HISTORY, PARTY, AND DIRECT CONTACTS ON VOTER TURNOUT

	OHIO	MARYLAND	PENNSYLVANIA	CALIFORNIA	ALL FOUR STATES
Total Contacts	0.02*	0.09**	0.03*	0.15**	0.065**
	(.01)	(.01)	(.02)	(.006)	(.01)
Voting History	0.83**	0.82**	0.63**	0.7**	0.74**
	(.03)	(.01)	(.02)	(.02)	(.01)
Age	0.01**	0.01**	0.01**	0.003*	0.007**
	(.001)	(.01)	(.01)	(.003)	(.01)
Democrat	1.02**	–0.3**	0.05*	–.1010*	0.182**
	(.07)	(.06)	(.07)	(.06)	(.05)
Republican	1.43**	–0.34*	0.31**	0.411**	0.384**
	(.07)	(.11)	(.07)	(.06)	(.04)
Presidential Year	—	—	—	—	0.483**
					(.04)
Constant	–2.08	–1.54**	–0.96	–1.27	–1.599**
	(.07)	(.09)	(.08)	(.06)	(.06)
N	11,333	17,264	14,974	14,848	22,830
Percent Predicted Correctly	77%	74%	73%	79%	74%
–2 Log Likelihood	11,275	13,470	14,269	16,318	18,560

Note: These equations were used to produce the partial effects in Table 6-3. Standard errors in parentheses.
**Significant at .01 level. *Significant at .05 (one-tail tests).

TABLE A-2 FACTORS AFFECTING VOTER TURNOUT
AMONG HABITUAL AND INFREQUENT VOTERS

	OHIO		MARYLAND		PENNSYLVANIA		CALIFORNIA	
	HABITUAL	INFREQUENT	HABITUAL	INFREQUENT	HABITUAL	INFREQUENT	HABITUAL	INFREQUENT
Total Contacts	-0.01	-0.013	0.065**	0.102***	-0.055*	0.074***	0.036**	0.197***
	(.02)	(.01)	(.03)	(.03)	(.03)	(.02)	(.05)	(.01)
Voting History	0.64***	0.74	0.824***	0.487***	0.658***	0.245***	0.935***	0.41***
	(.07)	(.05)	(.04)	(.06)	(.04)	(.05)	(.01)	(.06)
Age	0.008***	0.01	0.003***	0.015***	0.02***	0.007***	0.01***	0.002
	(.01)	(.01)	(.01)	(.01)	(.01)	(.01)	(.01)	(.01)
Democrat	1.35	0.64	-0.8***	-0.227**	0.335*	-0.03	0.154	-0.24***
	(.11)	(.10)	(.15)	(.07)	(.15)	(.08)	(.11)	(.07)
Republican	1.76	1.1	-0.81***	-0.27	0.46**	0.271***	0.389***	0.39***
	(.1)	(.09)	(.2)	(.15)	(.15)	(.08)	(.12)	(.07)
Constant	-1.87	-1.74	-0.57**	-1.64***	-1.44	-0.721	-1.7***	-1.34***
	(.1)	(.16)	(.2)	(.12)	(.18)	(.12)	(.19)	(.09)
N	5,245	6,088	7,229	7,894	8,340	5,940	7,985	6,014
Percent Predicted	74%	79%	84%	63%	86%	56%	89%	66%
-2 Log Likelihood	5,773	5,436	5,722	7,680	6,078	8,105	4,901	7,556

Note: These equations were used to produce the partial effects in Table 6-4. Habitual voters are defined as those who voted in two or more elections; infrequent voters are defined as those who voted in one or no elections. ***Significant at .001. **Significant at .01. *Significant at .05 (one-tail tests).

NOTES

1. Dwight Morris and Sara Fritz, *Handbook of Campaign Spending: Money in the 1990 Congressional Races* (Washington, DC: CQ Press, 1992), 11.
2. Ron Faucheaux, "Direct Mail," *Campaigns & Elections*, May 1997, 15.
3. Paul S. Herrnson, *Congressional Elections: Campaigning at Home and in Washington*, 2nd ed. (Washington, DC: CQ Press, 1998), 199.
4. Michael T. Hannahan, *Motivational Messages* (Unpublished dissertation, University of Massachusetts at Amherst, 1999), 62–63.
5. Richard Schlackman, then president of Campaign Performance Group, personal interview, December, 1996.
6. For a summary on voter information shortcuts, see Samuel L. Popkin, *The Reasoning Voter: Communication and Persuasion in Presidential Campaigns*, 2nd ed. (Chicago: University of Chicago Press, 1994), 44–71.
7. Patrick Sellers, "Strategy and Background in Congressional Campaigns," *American Political Science Review* 92 (1998): 159–171.
8. Stephen Ansolabehere and Shanto Iyengar, "Riding the Wave and Claiming Ownership Over Issues: The Joint Effects of Advertising and News Coverage in Campaigns," *Public Opinion Quarterly* 58 (1994): 335–337; John R. Petrocik, "Issue Ownership in Presidential Elections, with a 1980 Case Study," *American Journal of Political Science* 40 (1996): 825–850.
9. Herrnson, *Congressional Elections*, 177.
10. The notion of messages varying by competitiveness can be found in Stergios Skaperdas and Bernard Grofman, "Modeling Negative Campaigning," *American Political Science Review* 89 (1995): 49–61.
11. Herrnson, *Congressional Elections*, 171; Sellers, "Strategy and Background," 160.
12. Herrnson, *Congressional Elections*, 170–171; Kathleen Hall Jamieson, *Dirty Politics* (New York: Oxford University Press, 1992), 103; Daniel Shea, *Campaign Craft: The Strategies, Tactics, and Art of Political Campaign Management* (Westport, CT: Praeger, 1996), 10–15.
13. Stephen Hess, *The Little Book of Campaign Etiquette* (Washington, DC: Brookings Institute Press, 1998), 5.
14. Steve Meyers, English's direct-mail consultant, provided copies of the mailings.
15. Herrnson, *Congressional Elections*, 166.
16. For the classic statement on the costs and benefits of voting, see Anthony Downs, *An Economic Theory of Democracy* (New York: Harper & Row, 1957), 13, 80, 220.
17. Herbert F. Weisberg and Bernard Grofman, "Candidate Evaluations and Turnout," *American Politics Quarterly* 9 (1981): 197–219.
18. William H. Flanigan and Nancy H. Zingale, *Political Behavior of the American Electorate*, 4th ed. (Boston: Allyn and Bacon, 1979), 191–193.
19. Popkin, *The Reasoning Voter*, 38–42.
20. Popkin, *The Reasoning Voter*, 43.
21. Hannahan, *Motivational Messages*, 157–162.

7

ELECTIONS ARE MORE
THAN JUST A GAME

PAUL S. HERRNSON

Congressional elections are like virtually every other competition in that they have winners and losers, but they differ in that elections have an impact on public policy and thus have the potential to significantly alter people's lives. What implications do the lessons presented in the previous chapters have for representation and accountability in Congress and for the governmental process in general? What are the prospects for improving the quality of congressional elections formally, through enacting new regulations, and informally, through improving campaign conduct? This chapter addresses these questions.

FROM STARTING LINE TO FINISH LINE

Individuals consider running for Congress for a variety of reasons. Some feel deeply about specific issues and want to influence public policy. The psychological makeup of others encourages them to pursue positions that bring considerable power. Others wish to enjoy the prestige associated with holding a high-ranking political office. Some politicians run for Congress because it is the next step on a well-defined career ladder.[1] Regardless of their motives, it goes without saying that candidates and potential candidates for Congress would rather win than lose. Most consider their victory prospects when deciding whether to run or to sit out the race.

Incumbency figures prominently into most potential candidates' assessments of the viability of their candidacies. As Maisel, Stone, and Maestas demonstrate, the near-invincibility of House members—both real and perceived—discourages many highly qualified candidates from challenging them.

Fund-raising demands and the disruption of their personal lives also are powerful disincentives. These factors discourage potential candidates who possess many of the personal and strategic qualifications associated with quality challengers from running for the House, resulting in many incumbents getting reelected with little or no opposition. In 1998 roughly three-quarters of all House incumbents were handed their party's nomination without having to weather a primary challenge, and about one-fifth were returned to their seats without having to campaign against a major-party opponent in the general election. Substantially more incumbents faced challengers who lacked the personal or strategic skills and resources to mount anything approaching a competitive campaign.

Incumbency does more than influence who runs for Congress. It affects almost all, if not all, aspects of congressional campaigns, including the money candidates raise and spend, the kinds of campaign organizations they assemble, the tone and focus of their communications, and the techniques they use to convey their messages to voters. Incumbents possess tremendous advantages in raising contributions from virtually every type of congressional donor, including party committees, PACs, and individuals. Webster, Wilcox, Herrnson, Francia, Green, and Powell's study of the backgrounds, contribution and solicitation patterns, and motives of individuals who make large donations to congressional candidates shows that many of these donors make campaign contributions for reasons related to political access, including a desire to advance or protect the interests of their industry or to influence Congress. Because incumbents already occupy positions of power and are expected to maintain them, they receive the vast majority of contributions given by access-oriented donors. Donors who make contributions because they wish to advance a salient issue or a broad-based ideology also tend to favor incumbents because more incumbents than challengers have been in a position to establish a legislative track record in support of highly visible causes. Even individuals who contribute because they belong to a donor network or because they have a personal connection to a candidate are more likely to support an incumbent. By mere virtue of holding office, incumbents have had the opportunity to build larger donor networks and to become known by more political activists and voters.

Candidates who can amass larger war chests are able to field more formidable campaign organizations. Abbe, Herrnson, Magleby, and Patterson's analysis reveals that having the wherewithal to hire a team of professional campaign staffers and political consultants is yet another advantage of incumbency. Candidates who assemble the most formidable campaign teams also amass the most votes. Nevertheless, there are some downsides to the professionalization of congressional campaigns besides skyrocketing campaign costs. Political consultants bring their own norms and values to campaigns, and some of these can be harmful to the political process.[2] Candidates who rely

on teams of campaign professionals also are more likely to attack their opponents than those who rely on the help of political amateurs.

However, campaign professionalism is not the only factor that influences
the tone of a political campaign. The candidate's status is also relevant. Challengers are more likely to attack their opponents than are incumbents. Many
use negative campaign messages to try to peel off some of the incumbent's
base of voter support. Yet this strategy rarely results in a challenger's picking
up a significant number of votes.

Television is one of the most expensive and important tools congressional candidates use to communicate with voters. Despite the contributions that
televised ads make toward informing the electorate about candidates and issues, TV advertising has been criticized by many because of the rise of short
attack ads. Goldstein, Krasno, Bradford, and Seltz demonstrate that critics
have overstated the extent to which candidates attack their opponents on television. They show that only about one-quarter of the ads aired by candidates
in the 1998 congressional elections were pure attack ads. Roughly half were
positive ads, and the remaining quarter contrasted the candidates' issue positions. Incumbents, who have records of accomplishment to run on and defend, are less likely to sling mud at their opponents than are challengers, who
attack their opponents in order to give voters a reason to abandon their previous pro-incumbent election choices. Candidates in hotly contested elections
broadcast more negative TV ads than do those in one-sided contests, presumably because they believe that going negative is necessary to win in a
close race.

Of course, party committees and interest groups do not stand idly by and
watch the candidates they support compete for votes. The rise of issue advocacy spending, which is usually financed, at least in part, with soft money
raised outside of the federal laws that govern campaign finance, has increased
the roles of parties and groups in congressional elections. Candidates and
their parties appear to have created a *de facto* division of labor in the air wars
that define much of contemporary congressional election campaigns. Part of
the reason that candidates keep most of their TV ads positive is that the rise
of issue advocacy has enabled party committees to assume much of the responsibility for tearing down their opponents.

Hannahan's research on direct voter contact took the reader from the air
war to the ground war, showing that direct mail, telemarketing, and fieldwork are also important forms of campaign communications. Their major advantages are that they are less expensive than television advertising and that
they can be more precisely targeted to individual voters. Another advantage
is that direct voter contact has a measurable impact: The more contacts an individual receives, the more likely he or she is to actually cast a vote.

Campaigns spend most of the dollars they invest in voter contact to reach
habitual voters. Their goal is to try to ensure that these individuals turn out
to support their candidate on election day. Given these individuals' already

strong propensities to go to the polls, such contacts have relatively little impact on their voting behavior. Ironically, direct voter contact has a much greater impact on infrequent voters, who are the least likely to receive them. Campaign strategy clearly contributes to low levels of voter turnout in congressional elections.

Collectively, the studies in this volume demonstrate that the current system of congressional elections is governed by a set of rules, norms, and expectations that is not neutral. The system bestows tremendous advantages on members of Congress who seek reelection. Indeed, more than 90 percent of all these individuals win, and the vast majority of them defeat their opponents by margins in excess of 20 percent of the vote. The congressional election system, however, does not guarantee that every incumbent will automatically win. Nor does it prescribe a singular path to victory that all incumbents follow or a route to defeat that all challengers are destined to take. Instead, the system gives incumbents, challengers, and open-seat contestants tremendous leeway in deciding how they will wage their campaigns. The pressure to win results in some campaigns attacking their opponents personally or restricting their outreach efforts to limited groups of voters. These strategies may be politically expedient, but they are not good for the political system.

AFTER THE RACE

The desire to win and hold on to political office does not evaporate once an elected official is sworn into office. Members of Congress are charged with governing the nation, but their attention rarely turns from election politics. House members' two-year terms encourage them to devote significant amounts of time and effort to building relationships with voters and preparing for their reelection campaigns. They develop "home styles"—ways of relating to voters—to help them forge bonds of trust with their constituents.[3] They also cultivate relationships with previous and potential campaign contributors. Legislators recognize that those who ignore their district-based reelection constituency, or fail to cultivate their more national financial constituency, do so at their peril.

The impact that legislators' preoccupations with reelection have on the modern Congress goes beyond their devoting substantial time and energy to the "permanent campaign." Members have seen to it that Congress provides them with resources that help them to perpetuate their legislative careers. The House provides each member with a Capitol Hill office, funds to rent and furnish one or more district offices, and a lavish set of accounts for hiring aides, traveling back and forth to the district, and corresponding with constituents—resources that have a combined value of more than $1 million annually.[4] Both the House and the Senate, and the Democratic and Republican congressional campaign committees, own television and radio studios that members use to communicate with voters and the general public. The campaign committees furnish House members with other useful election resources, including telephone suites, meeting rooms, and contributor lists for use in fund-raising.[5]

Members are prohibited from using congressional resources to raise money or solicit votes, but they can use these to increase their visibility and popularity with supporters. Most legislators routinely send general, targeted, and personalized letters, as well as newsletters, to constituents in order to advertise their activities, claim credit for helping constituents and bringing federal projects to the district, and publicize popular policy stances.[6] Legislators also use the influence over the policymaking process that comes with their office as a fund-raising tool. Party leaders and committee leaders, policy entrepreneurs, members of influential committees, and even first-term representatives are able to identify individuals and PACs whose interests they can influence and from whom they can collect contributions.[7] Donors recognize that their contributions bring them some political benefits, including an increased likelihood that they will be able to meet with members to discuss specific public policies.[8] Of course, access is an essential first step toward influence in the policymaking process.

The fact that members of Congress are largely responsible for their tenure in office gives them tremendous room to maneuver when participating in the legislative process. The election system encourages legislators to be hyperresponsive to voters' viewpoints on highly salient issues, and to be attentive to the positions of party leaders, committee chairs, congressional policy experts, and campaign contributors and lobbyists on others. Moreover, the same campaign system that forces candidates to put themselves, not their party, first when running for office encourages most House members to devote more time to advancing their individual political careers than their party's collective goals. Even the party leaders who are entrusted with building legislative coalitions advise their colleagues to vote against their party's position on particular bills if supporting them will endanger their chances to get reelected.[9] Party unity on congressional roll-call votes is more a function of a member's ideology and the distribution of partisan voters in his or her district than of the persuasive abilities of party leaders.[10] Incumbent-dominated candidate-centered elections enable individual legislators to work first and foremost to promote the interests of their supporters. Allegiances to party leaders and national party platforms almost always take a back seat.

Members' independent streaks and pressures arising from constituents, contributors, and the myriad of interest-group lobbyists who compete for influence results in a decentralized Congress—one that is better at airing public issues and dealing with short-term crises than at engaging in long-range policymaking. These same forces also often result in Congress's passing watered-down omnibus bills that contain something for everyone rather than targeted legislation that is designed to address specific problems. This has opened up

Congress to the criticism that it engages in wasteful spending and has contributed to the national debt.

Critics of the current congressional election system maintain that it unfairly favors incumbents, wealthy candidates, and individuals and groups that can afford to spend large amounts in campaigns. Detractors further charge that campaigns appear to involve more mudslinging than meaningful discussion of the issues. They also point out that some campaign communications are so targeted that they are more exclusive than inclusive in terms of the voters they ultimately reach. Another serious indictment of the system is that the financial costs, personal investment, and rough-and-tumble of campaigning discourage many individuals who would make good legislators from running for Congress. Political reformers have argued that these and other shortcomings in the campaign system warrant introducing a host of election reforms, ranging from term limits to campaign finance reform to voluntary measures, such as the adoption of codes of campaign conduct.

Term limits have been passed in more than a dozen states, but their constitutionality remains in question. Their supporters maintain that term limits would result in a rotation of "citizen legislators" who would be willing to spend a few years working to resolve the nation's problems and then return home. Term limits supporters tout these individuals as the cure for the twin evils of gridlock and unnecessary government spending. They believe that because term-limited legislators are neither entrenched politicians nor people who are interested in pursuing full-time political careers, they would be more open to compromise when making policy and would be uninterested in spending government funds for the purpose of helping themselves get reelected.[11]

Detractors of the term limits movement counter that even though they would result in a greater rotation among House members, they more than likely would result in the election of experienced politicians and wealthy citizens, who can raise the money needed to wage a campaign, not citizen legislators. Many of these individuals would probably be just as concerned with their post-congressional professional lives as with governing the nation. Their lack of experience or knowledge of the issues and legislative process would inevitably result in their relying heavily on the judgment of congressional staff, executive-branch aides, lobbyists, and other members of the Washington establishment. Moreover, because most highly qualified challengers would prefer to wait for a House seat to become open rather than face the long odds of defeating an incumbent, term limits would probably reduce electoral competition and limit incumbent accountability.

Congressional term limits can only be enacted by a simple but politically demanding measure, the passage of a Constitutional amendment. The Republicans tried to enact a term limits amendment following their historic takeover of Congress in 1994, but they fell short of the two-thirds majority necessary in the House and the Senate. The argument that term limits are needed to ensure turnover in Congress has been overtaken by congressional turnover itself: Almost 6 of 10 members of the 106th Congress took office after the 1990 elections.[12]

The Federal Election Campaign Act (FECA) has not reduced the influence of money in elections, decreased the influence of wealthy individuals and groups in political campaigns, or encouraged more people to participate in the financing of congressional elections. It has contributed to an election system that pits under-funded challengers against extremely well-financed incumbents. Very few challengers possess the resources needed to hold an incumbent accountable for his or her record in office.

Moreover, the law has been weakened since it was last amended in 1979. Congressional candidates, political consultants, party officials, interest-group leaders, and some of the most astute legal minds in the United States have located loopholes in the law, stretched them beyond recognition, and successfully challenged many campaign finance regulations in the courts and at the Federal Election Commission. The boldness of some of these individuals is encapsulated in Republican pollster Frank Luntz's predictions for the 2000 elections: "You're going to see ads that just manage to skirt the edge of legality. The motto will be, 'Put it all out there, and let the lawyers fight about it later.'"[13] The willingness of Luntz and others to override various aspects of the FECA is indicative of the natural aging cycle of a regulatory regime.[14] Another part of that cycle involves the legislative process: Lawmakers are normally expected to pass laws that shore up aspects of regulatory regimes that have been weakened and replace those that have been eviscerated. At this point, the regulatory regime governing campaign finance is almost as much loophole as law.

Why hasn't Congress succeeded in reforming the campaign finance system? Members have introduced several dozen bills proposing to "fix" the system in each session, and the House has recently passed some bills only to have them fail in the Senate. Campaign finance reform is an issue that divides politicians by partisanship, ideology, and for pragmatic reasons. Most Democrats believe that the role of money in elections should be minimized. Many favor combining strict campaign contribution and spending limits with cash subsidies or free or low-cost access to television, radio, or postage. Most Republicans are opposed to restricting the flow of campaign cash and using taxpayer dollars or federally regulated airways to subsidize campaign communications. Some believe that limiting campaign spending is a violation of First Amendment free speech rights, and that subsidizing campaign communications would constitute an unwarranted government intrusion into the telecommunications market. The parties' positions reflect their underlying ideologies and beliefs about what kind of campaign finance system would work to their candidates' advantage. Most Republicans embrace a free market ideology, and their party raises more money than does the Democratic Party. Most Democrats believe that government plays a positive role in subsidizing presidential elections and many other political and economic endeavors, and they recognize that reforms that equalize the funding available to both parties work to their advantage.

House–Senate differences, geography, and demography also have an impact on legislators' opinions on campaign reform. Members of the two chambers tend to hold different views, in part because they draw their funds from different sources and face different fund-raising pressures. Senate candidates raise and spend much more than do their House counterparts, and they raise their funds over a longer period. Senate candidates depend more on individual contributions and less on PAC dollars. Candidates from poor states, women, minorities, and others from traditionally underrepresented groups raise more money across state borders than do white men from wealthy areas.

Of course, some of the biggest differences of opinion over what, if any, form of campaign finance reform is most desirable is based on incumbency. Members of Congress recognize that they directly benefit from the biases in the existing campaign finance system, and most oppose making changes that would increase their opponent's ability to compete against them. Many congressional challengers take strong stands on reform issues, but their policy stances are of little import because they are in no position to change the law and they frequently change their views once they get elected to office. In short, one of the major difficulties in passing campaign finance reform is that incumbents know which aspects of the current system work to their advantage, and they recognize that any reform measure that is enacted will probably have a direct impact on their prospects for political survival.

Other reforms that affect the congressional election system can be, and have been, introduced at the state level. Some states have laws that ease the burdens imposed on citizens who wish to vote. Wisconsin, Maine, and five other states have same-day registration, which allows citizens to register to vote immediately before casting their ballots. Oregon allows individuals to vote by mail. Seventeen other states have liberal absentee balloting procedures. Texas allows individuals to vote before election day at any location in their county, including at mobile polling places. Arizona pioneered computerized voting when in March 2000 some of its citizens voted in the state's Democratic primary via the Internet. The Arizona experiment led voters to cast 39,942 ballots—more than 46 percent of the total—through cyberspace, but it soon came under challenge in the courts because it increased the electoral access of wealthy persons who owned computers over poorer voters.[15] Partisanship, political philosophy, and the same kinds of political considerations that pose hurdles to federal campaign finance reform make it unlikely that all of the states with demanding registration and voting requirements will soon allow their citizens to benefit from flexible voting procedures such as these. However, state leaders regularly follow developments in their sister states, and some of these innovations are likely to be adopted on a more widespread basis.

Other aspects of the congressional election system are beyond regulation. The number of debates scheduled, the individuals and specific groups targeted for voter communications, and the tenor of those communications are all strategic decisions that lie beyond the purview of most governments. Nevertheless, some candidates are so fed up with the pressures of fund-raising, attack ads, and the absence of a meaningful dialogue in most political communications that they negotiate agreements with their opponents to improve the quality of their specific election. Some of these pacts are reached privately between the campaigns themselves. In 1998, for example, Senate incumbent Russell Feingold (D-WI) and his Republican challenger, Representative Mark Neumann, agreed to limit their spending to $3.8 million each—one dollar per Wisconsin voter—and both stuck close to the bargain.[16]

The most effective agreements are usually initiated or mediated by outside organizations, such as the Alliance for Better Campaigns and the Project on Campaign Conduct. These organizations seek to promote high ethical standards for candidates and improve the quality of media election coverage. The Alliance was involved in ten 1998 gubernatorial elections, encouraging the candidates to participate in debates, appear in their ads, and refrain from making false or misleading attacks on their opponents. It also encouraged media organizations to conduct "ad watches" so that they could hold candidates accountable for their television commercials by informing the public about their accuracy.[17] The Project on Campaign Conduct focused its efforts on Ohio and Washington, and had a major impact on the House race between Representative Jack Metcalf (R-WA) and Margarethe Cammermeyer, his Democratic challenger.[18] Although these organizations concentrated their efforts on a limited number of races, other groups have encouraged and will continue to encourage candidates for Congress and other offices to sign codes of conduct.

Given that the prospects for reforming the campaign system through legal channels appear bleak, the willingness of candidates and groups to adopt codes of conduct has taken on greater significance. Nevertheless, the impact of such codes is limited because of their voluntary nature. It is unlikely that codes of conduct will be initiated in most elections, and they are most likely to be rejected by candidates and political consultants who could use the guidance the most. Moreover, codes of conduct are likely to break down when they are needed most—when increasing competition causes a race to heat up. In the midst of any hard-fought contest, whether it be a congressional campaign or a baseball game, competitors who have signed agreements with the best of intentions may ultimately break them because they are advised that it is the only way they can win and because they recognize that they face no sanctions for doing so. Codes of conduct have the potential to improve congressional elections, but they are not a substitute for meaningful campaign reform, especially in congressional elections, where most contestants are used to playing hardball.

NOTES

1. Joseph A. Schlessinger, *Ambition and Politics: Political Careers in the United States* (Chicago: Rand McNally, 1996), 99; David T. Canon, *Actors, Athletes, and Astronauts* (Chicago: University of Chicago Press, 1990), 50–53, 56–58.

2. James A. Thurber, Candice J. Nelson, and David A. Dulio, "The Consultants Speak: An Analysis of Campaign Professionals' Attitudes," paper presented at a Conference on the Role of Consultants in Elections, Washington, DC, June 19, 1998.

3. Richard F. Fenno Jr., *Home Style: House Members in Their Districts* (Boston: Little, Brown, 1978), 54–61.

4. The figures are for 1999. See Roger H. Davidson and Walter J. Oleszek, *Congress and Its Members* (Washington, DC: CQ Press, 2000), 154.

5. Paul S. Herrnson, *Congressional Elections: Campaigning at Home and in Washington*, 3rd ed. (Washington, DC: CQ Press, 2000), 105–109; Herrnson, *Party Campaigning in the 1980s* (Cambridge, MA: Harvard University Press, 1988), ch. 3.

6. David R. Mayhew, *Congress: The Electoral Connection* (New Haven: Yale University Press, 1974); Morris P. Fiorina, *Congress: Keystone of the Washington Establishment* (New Haven: Yale University Press, 1978), 19–21, 41–49, 56–62; Diane E. Yiannakis, "The Grateful Electorate: Casework and Congressional Elections," *American Journal of Political Science* 25 (1981): 568–580; Bruce Cain, John Ferejohn, and Morris Fiorina, *The Personal Vote* (Cambridge, MA: Harvard University Press, 1987), 103–106; Gary C. Jacobson, *The Politics of Congressional Elections*, 4th ed. (New York: Longman, 1997), 28–33; George Serra and Albert Cover, "The Electoral Consequences of Perquisite Use: The Casework Case," *Legislative Studies Quarterly* 17 (1992): 233–246.

7. Herrnson, *Congressional Elections*, 160.

8. Laura Langbein, "Money and Access: Some Empirical Evidence," *Journal of Politics* 48 (1986): 1052–1062; Richard Hall and Frank Wayman, "Buying Time: Moneyed Interests and the Mobilization of Bias in Congressional Committees," *American Political Science Review* 84 (1990): 797–820.

9. Herrnson, *Congressional Elections*, 256.

10. See, for example, Herbert F. Weisberg, "Evaluating Theories of Congressional Roll Call Voting," *American Journal of Political Science* (1978): 554–577.

11. See, for example, John H. Fund, "Term Limitation: An Idea Whose Time Has Come," in Gerald Benjamin and Michael J. Malbin, eds., *Limiting Legislative Terms* (Washington, DC: CQ Press, 1992), 230.

12. Charles R. Kesler, "Bad Housekeeping: The Case against Congressional Term Limits," in Benjamin and Malbin, 246–248; Herrnson, *Congressional Elections*, 266.

13. Dick Polman, "No Rest in the Battle between Bush, Gore," *Philadelphia Inquirer*, March 9, 2000.

14. Frank J. Sorauf, *Inside Campaign Finance* (New Haven: Yale University Press, 1992), 56–57.

15. Ben White, "Online Balloting: A Question of Fairness," *Washington Post*, March 19, 2000.

16. Clyde Wilcox, "They Did It Their Way: Campaign Finance Principles and Realities Clash in Wisconsin 1998, Sen. Russell Feingold (D) vs. Rep. Mark Neumann (R)," in Michael A. Bailey, Ronald A. Faucheaux, Paul S. Herrnson, and Clyde Wilcox, eds., *Campaigns & Elections: Contemporary Case Studies* (Washington, DC: CQ Press, 1999), 45–46.

17. Peggy Anderson, "Coming Clean: Election Campaigns Can Be Truthful, Accurate, Informative, and Issue-Oriented and Hard-Hitting," *Trust Magazine* (Philadelphia: The Pew Charitable Trusts, 1999).

18. Brad Rourke, "Taking the Pledge: Codes of Conduct," *Campaigns & Elections* 20, August, 1999.

INDEX